iPhone 14
SENIORS GUIDE

THE BEGINNER'S PATHWAY TO EASILY MASTER YOUR NEW IPHONE'S WONDERS IN NO TIME, WITH ILLUSTRATED AND EASY-TO-FOLLOW INSTRUCTIONS

Arthur Pylon

GET YOUR BONUS NOW!

The BONUSES below are **100% FREE**, and all you need to get it is a name and an email address. **It's super simple!**

BONUS #1
THE ULTIMATE APP GUIDE FOR SENIORS

BONUS #2
PRESERVING YOUR IPHONE:
MAINTENANCE AND UPKEEP FOR THE LONG RUN

BONUS #3
DECODING TECH TALK:
A GLOSSARY FOR THE MODERN SENIOR

TO DOWNLOAD IT SCAN
THE QR CODE BELOW OR GO TO

http://bonusforbooks.com/arthur-pylon-iq

SCAN ME

Table of Contents

Overview of Topics Covered in the Guidebook

Welcome to the guidebook for the **iPhone 14**, tailor-made to help individuals like you who are new to the device and eager to maximize its potential. This comprehensive manual offers a wide array of information, empowering you with the knowledge and expertise to efficiently navigate and utilize the iPhone 14's features.

In the first chapter, we delve into the evolution of smartphones, highlighting the iPhone's groundbreaking impact on the mobile industry. **We specifically focus on how the iPhone 14 benefits seniors, emphasizing its user-friendly interface, accessibility features, and a multitude of tools designed to enhance your daily life**. As the chapter concludes, we provide an overview of the guidebook's contents, giving you a glimpse into the valuable insights and skills you can expect to acquire.

Chapter 2 dives into understanding the iPhone 14 itself. **We'll discuss the different models and variants available, such as the iPhone 14, 14 Plus, 14 Pro, and 14 Pro Max**. You'll get acquainted with the physical features and buttons of the device, allowing you to navigate effortlessly. We'll also explore the Home screen and app layout, enabling you to personalize your iPhone 14 and make it suit your preferences and needs.

Getting started with your iPhone is the focus of Chapter 3. We'll walk you through the unboxing process and guide you on setting up your iPhone 14, **ensuring a smooth and seamless experience**. You'll learn how to create an Apple ID and an iCloud account, which will enable you to access various Apple services and securely store your data. We'll also cover connecting to Wi-Fi and cellular networks, allowing you to stay connected wherever you go. Personalizing your iPhone 14 settings and preferences is another important aspect covered in this chapter, empowering you to tailor your device to your liking.

Chapter 4 is all about **communication made easy on your iPhone 14**. You'll discover how to make and receive phone calls effortlessly, explore the messaging features and apps for sending and receiving text messages, and learn how to manage your contacts and favorites effectively. We'll specifically delve into popular messaging apps like iMessage and WeChat, highlighting their features and how you can make the most of them.

Capturing and managing photos is the focus of Chapter 5. **We'll guide you on using the Camera app to take stunning photos**, and we'll explore editing and enhancing those photos directly on your iPhone 14. Organizing and sharing your photos through the Photos app will also be covered, along with using iCloud Photos for backup and synchronization.

Chapter 6 introduces you to **useful apps and tools specifically tailored for seniors**. You'll come across health and fitness applications that will help you keep active and track your health. We'll also explore productivity and organization apps that enhance your daily life and entertainment and media streaming apps that provide you with hours of enjoyment.

In Chapter 7, we'll explore the **accessibility features available on the iPhone 14, designed to enhance usability for individuals with visual or hearing impairments**. You'll learn about VoiceOver and Zoom, powerful tools that provide audio feedback and magnification for easier interaction with your device. We'll also provide tips for enhancing visual and hearing accessibility on your iPhone 14.

Chapter 8 **focuses on online safety and security**. You'll learn how to protect your personal information online, recognize and avoid common scams, and configure privacy settings on your iPhone 14. We'll also provide tips for creating and managing strong passwords, ensuring the security of your online accounts.

Troubleshooting and support are covered in Chapter 9. We'll address common issues and **provide troubleshooting solutions to help you overcome any challenges you may encounter**. You'll also learn how to reset your iPhone 14 and restore data when needed, as well as discover various Apple support resources and authorized service providers to seek assistance when necessary.

In Chapter 10, we'll delve into **advanced tips and tricks to enhance your iPhone 14** experience. You'll uncover hidden features and shortcuts for efficient usage, master Siri for voice commands and dictation, learn how to maximize battery life and optimize performance, and explore advanced camera functions and modes for capturing stunning photos and videos.

Lastly, Chapter 11 **emphasizes the importance of staying up to date with iOS updates**. You'll understand the benefits of installing software updates, learn how to check for and install updates on your iPhone 14, and explore the new features and improvements introduced with each update.

With this comprehensive guidebook, you'll become confident in using your iPhone 14 and harnessing its full potential. Let's embark on this journey together and unlock the remarkable capabilities of your iPhone 14!

CHAPTER 1: Introduction to the iPhone

The Evolution of Smartphones

The development of cellphones has proved to be a wonderful journey; they started out as simple devices for communication but have now evolved into formidable handheld computers which are now an essential component of our day-to-day life. In this introduction, we will explore the significant milestones in the evolution of smartphones, leading up to the iPhone 14.

The concept of a smartphone began to take shape in the early 1990s, with devices like the IBM Simon and Nokia Communicator series. These devices offered basic features such as email, fax, and rudimentary web browsing, but they were bulky and expensive, limiting their widespread adoption.

In 2000, Nokia introduced the Nokia 3310, a popular feature phone that laid the foundation for future advancements. However, it wasn't until 2007 when Apple revolutionized the smartphone industry with the release of the first iPhone. The original iPhone featured a touch-based interface, a mobile version of Safari for web browsing, and an App Store, setting the stage for a new era of smartphones.

Following the success of the iPhone, competitors like Samsung, HTC, and later Google entered the market with their Android-based smartphones, introducing features like customizable home screens, multitasking capabilities, and expandable storage options. This sparked a fierce rivalry between iOS and Android, which continues to shape the smartphone landscape today.

Over the years, smartphones underwent rapid evolution in terms of design, features, and performance. The introduction of high-resolution displays, faster processors, improved cameras, and increased storage capacities became standard across flagship devices. Additionally, the integration of sensors like accelerometers, gyroscopes, and

GPS opened up new possibilities for augmented reality (AR) and location-based services.

Another significant development was the rise of mobile apps. The App Store and Google Play Store became vast marketplaces, offering millions of applications that transformed smartphones into versatile tools for productivity, communication, entertainment, and more.

As smartphones progressed, they also became more interconnected. The advent of 4G networks enabled faster data speeds, paving the way for seamless video streaming, online gaming, and cloud-based services. With the emergence of 5G technology, smartphones gained access to even faster speeds, low latency, and improved network capacity, enabling advancements in areas like virtual reality (VR) and Internet of Things (IoT) integration.

Now, let's fast forward to the iPhone 14, which represents the culmination of years of innovation and technological advancements. While specific details about the iPhone 14 may not be available as of my knowledge cutoff in September 2021, we can anticipate several potential developments based on the trends observed in recent years.

The iPhone 14 could feature further improvements in processing power, camera capabilities, and display technology, providing users with an enhanced multimedia experience. It may also include biometric authentication technologies like as under-display fingerprint sensors or enhanced face recognition algorithms.

Additionally, we might see advancements in battery technology, aiming to provide longer-lasting battery life. Furthermore, the integration of 5G connectivity will likely be standard, allowing for faster and more reliable network speeds.

In terms of design, the iPhone 14 might continue the trend of minimizing bezels and maximizing screen real estate, possibly adopting a sleeker and more streamlined form factor. Materials used could evolve to offer improved durability and aesthetics.

Furthermore, the iPhone 14 could leverage advancements in AI and ML to deliver more tailored and context-aware experiences, such as smarter voice assistants and improved predictive capabilities.

Overall, the evolution of smartphones up to the iPhone 14 showcases the relentless pursuit of innovation in the mobile industry. As technology continues to advance, smartphones are expected to become even more powerful, seamlessly integrated into our lives, and serving as gateways to a connected world.

Benefits of Using an iPhone 14 for Seniors

It is often assumed that young people will profit the most from mobile phone use. However, one-quarter of the over-65 population lacks one. Given that the vast majority of today's American children learn to operate a phone before they learn to communicate on one, this is quite surprising. Fortunately, statistics show that a rising number of pensioners are buying cell phones.

Giving your parents a mobile phone may be a considerate present that serves multiple objectives, including safeguarding their safety and keeping in touch with you and other family members. Consider just five of the numerous advantages that mobile phones like iPhone 14 provide.

- **Help in Times of Need**

Aging parents are more likely to experience a number of unanticipated medical issues, such as accidents, falls, heart attacks, and strokes. The main benefit of smartphones is that they make it easy and quick for the elderly to call for help. Even if they are unable to contact you directly, many programs can be configured to tell you instantly if they encounter a problem.

- **Practice healthful practices on a regular basis.**

Apps for tracking health and fitness indicators such as blood pressure, heart rate, and BMI are now available for smartphones with and without contracts. These advancements allow seniors to store their medical records in an one spot.

- **Keep in touch with one's social group.**

Parents may communicate with their children at all times owing to mobile phones. While it may become more difficult to establish meaningful connections as we age, the finest phone plans (and inexpensive mobile phone plans) make it simpler.

- **Act as a source of distraction**

Smartphones can now do much more than just make and receive phone calls; they can also play media such as music, movies, and games. Almost every contemporary smartphone comes with fascinating extras that will keep your grandparents entertained.

- **Propose Some Downtime**

We are concerned about leaving our elderly parents behind, even though it is best for us. Your concerns about your elderly loved one's health and boredom may be alleviated if they have access to a cell phone.

CHAPTER 2: Understanding the iPhone

Introduction to the iPhone 14 Models and Variants

Apple iPhone 14

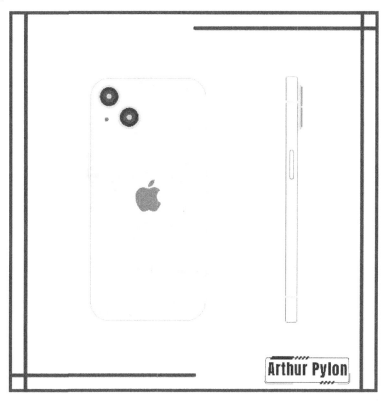

The iPhone 14 is maybe the smallest update we've seen in a while since it maintains the same design and basic technology, adding just the new Crash Detection function and removing the actual SIM card port in the US.

The Apple iPhone 14 is conservative in both aesthetic and hardware, making the iPhone 14 Pro's offer this year more appealing than it may have been in previous years.

Of course, there have been some advancements. The front camera is improved, the main camera is improved, and the battery is somewhat bigger than on the iPhone 13. Although there hasn't been much of a performance improvement and the design has remained the same, it is still a fantastic design.

Apple iPhone 14 Plus

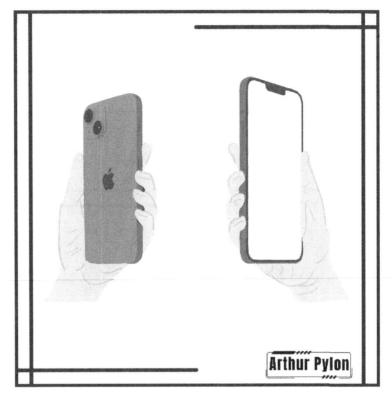

With a bigger display than the original model, Apple's iPhone 14 Plus represents a new approach for the company. With a 6.7-inch screen, it has the similar basic specifications as the iPhone 14. Apple discontinued the "small" from their iPhone quartet and introduced the huge, 6.7" iPhone 14 Plus in its stead.

The Apple iPhone 14 Plus brings an exciting new design to the standard iPhone lineup, offering a larger screen size without the premium price tag of the Pro models.

This makes it an excellent choice for individuals seeking a bigger display while still considering budget constraints.

However, as enthusiasts at Pocket-lint, we have a special fondness for the compact iPhone variant and feel a tinge of disappointment in not seeing a new small-sized iPhone this year.

Apple iPhone 14 Pro

The iPhone 14 Pro has the same appearance as the 13 Pro, but it is more powerful thanks to the A16 Bionic processor, a new 48-megapixel primary camera, and a new Dynamic Island notch.

Undoubtedly, among the four recently introduced iPhone 14 models, the Apple iPhone 14 Pro stands out as the most captivating option. Boasting a refreshed design, it brings forth notable advancements in terms of its camera, CPU performance, and display technology. Furthermore, there are reports of an extended battery life, and the inclusion of the impressive Dynamic Island feature ensures that battery improvements are something we can all appreciate. With its multitude of enhancements, the Apple iPhone 14 Pro truly piques our interest and sets itself apart as an enticing choice.

Apple iPhone 14 Pro Max

Everything about the iPhone 14 Pro is carried over to the bigger, 6.7-inch display of the iPhone 14 Pro Max. The new cameras, all the power, and the Dynamic Island experience are yours as a result.

The Apple iPhone 14 Pro Max is large in both shape and personality. Along with speed improvements, battery improvements, camera upgrades, the Always-On Display, and the Dynamic Island feature, there is a new design that is truly attractive, particularly in this bigger version.

This smartphone is great for people who prefer a bigger screen or better battery life, even though it is rather hefty, pricey, and has all the same functionality as its smaller sister.

Exploring the Physical Features and Buttons

The iPhone 14 and 14 Plus

The iPhone 14 and 14 Plus are the most recent affordable smartphones from Apple in the iPhone 14 lineup. The company has discontinued the "Mini" version. Both models have screen sizes of 6.1 and 6.7 inches. The two devices are similar to the iPhone 13 models in that they have flat edges, an aerospace-grade aluminum chassis, and a glass back that allows for wireless charging.

The iPhone 14 and 14 Plus come in five different color options: midnight, blue, purple, starlight, and red.

Both devices retain the notch at the front of the screen, which houses the TrueDepth camera, as opposed to the 14 Pro models, which have the notch replaced with "Display Island."

The devices feature a Super Retina XDR OLED screen with up to 1200 nits of peak brightness, Dolby Vision, and True Tone, which adjusts the screen's white balance to the background lighting. Unlike the Pro models, the iPhone 14 and 14 Plus do not have ProMotion display technology.

The screen of the iPhone is shielded by a durable Ceramic Shield front cover, and the device is IP68 water resistant, permitting submersion at a depth of six meters for almost thirty mins.

Both low-cost models use the A15 chip, also used in the iPhone 13 lineup. On the other hand, Apple has improved internal design to allow for improved thermal performance. The processor has a six-core CPU, a five-core GPU, and a sixteen-core Neural Engine.

Apple has upgraded the iPhone 7 Plus's wide-angle camera to twelve megapixels, giving it a bigger sensor, a bigger aperture (/1.5), bigger pixels (1.9 m), and sensor-shift optical stabilization of the image for enhanced efficiency in low-light settings. They have also added an upgraded "TrueDepth" camera with an aperture of /1.9.

Additionally, even though the "Ultrawide" lens has not been changed, the Photonic Engine technology increases low-light shooting whilst utilizing the camera app.

Apple has also added Action Mode when recording videos to provide a polished look with improved photo stabilization. Don't worry if you need to record a video in the middle of the action; Action Mode can compensate for severe shaking, movements, and vibrations. Cinematic Mode has also been improved, allowing you to record in 4K at 30 frames per second (fps) and 4K at 24 fps. Surprisingly, the True Tone flash is now 10% brighter and more consistent.

The new Crash Detection feature is powered by a "dual-core accelerometer, an accelerometer, and a high dynamic range gyroscope." This feature allows you to notify emergency services in the event that you find yourself in a major accident but are unable to use your iPhone. The barometer analyzes deviates in cabin pressure, the GPS sensor monitors speed variations, and the microphone detects impact sounds similar to car crashes. This feature is also available in iPhone 14 Pro models.

For the first time, the Cupertino-based company has included Satellite Emergency SOS. This feature allows your iPhone to communicate with satellites when Wi-Fi and cellular networks are unavailable.

The Emergency SOS through satellite works in an open space without obstructing trees and lets you send texts to the emergency service. = In the Find My app, you can additionally utilize satellite connectivity to share your location with your pals and loved ones. As expected, this feature is also available in the Pro models

The iPhone 14 models support 5G connectivity. In the US, the device comes with an eSIM, while other regions can still ship with a physical SIM card slot. Apple has also enhanced the iPhone 14's battery life.

Both phones support MagSafe charging up to 15W and fast charging through Lightning with a 20W or higher charger.

It offers three storage options: 128GB, 256GB, and 512GB storage capacities. Both devices also support Wi-Fi 6 and Bluetooth 5.3.

The iPhone 14 Pro and 14 Pro Max

The iPhone 14 Pro and 14 Pro Max were unveiled alongside the cheaper 14 and 14 Plus. The Pro model offers more rich features than the iPhone 14 models, ranging from improved camera technology, an enhanced display, an even faster A16 processor, *etc.*

The iPhone 14 Pro has a 6.1-inch screen, whilst the Pro Max comes with a 6.7-inch. Both devices feature flat edges, a stainless-steel casing, IP68 water resistance, textured matte glass at the back, and a Ceramic Shield for screen protection.

It now has a larger camera bump to house the new lenses, and there are changes on display.

Apple has removed the notch that houses the TrueDepth camera technology and has rather adopted what the company called "Dynamic Island," which is a pill-shaped hole at the front of the phone's screen that contains the camera system and can get bigger or smaller, depending on what's showing on your screen.

The "Dynamic Island" now shows phone calls, reminders, timers, notifications, map directions, and activities in the location where the notch used to be.

Both devices have a refreshed Super Retina XDR display with improved ProMotion technology and an Always-On display. Your wallpaper is dimmed while the widgets, time, and other live activities are still available when Always-On Display is turned on. The screen also offers a maximum HDR brightness of up to 2000 nits.

The iPhone 14 Pro models are powered by the new A16 processor, which offers speed and performance improvements. The processor has a six-core CPU, an accelerated five-core GPU with 50% additional memory bandwidth, and a refreshed sixteen-core Neural Engine, which could whole 17 trillion operations per sec.

The Pro models now have a 48-MP wide camera fitted with a quad-pixel sensor that adapts to the image being taken. The devices can record at a full 48 MP with ProRAW, which allows the capture of professional images.

The TrueDepth front-facing camera now has an enhanced f/1.9 aperture for improved selfies and video shooting in a dark environment, and it has now included autofocus for the first time.

Apple has designed the Adaptive True Tone flash with a series of 9 LEDs that adjust patterns depending on the lens focal length. Other photographic features include Photographic Styles, Smart HDR 4, Portrait Mode, Night Mode, *etc.*

It offers four storage options: 128GB, 256GB, 512GB, and 1TB storage capacities. Both devices also support Wi-Fi 6 and Bluetooth 5.3.

The Pro models also support 5G connectivity, Massif charging up to 15W, and fast charging through Lightning with a 20W or higher charger.

Parts of the iPhone 14

To begin our journey, let's learn a few things about the parts of your new iPhone. The diagram below highlights the important parts you need to know.

Buttons: The iPhone has three important buttons, the Side button, and two volume buttons. The Side button is used to turn off your iPhone and lock and unlock it. The volume buttons on your iPhone are used to adjust the volume.

Ring/Silent Switch: This switch is used for rapidly muting (and unmuting) your phone. Simply push it backward to mute and forward to unmute the phone (for example, when you're in a meeting).

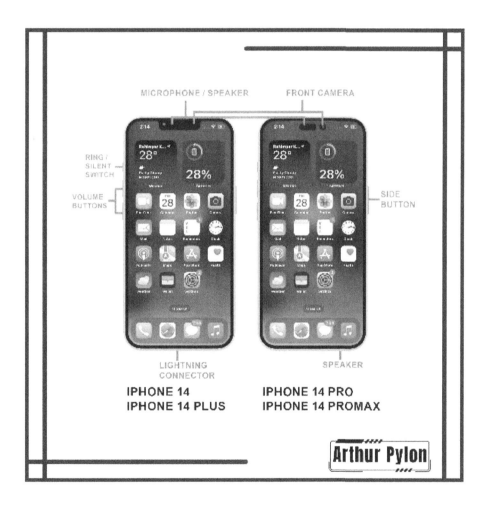

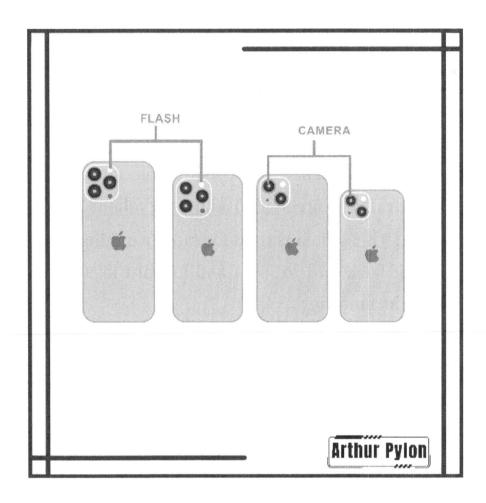

Cameras: There are two groups of cameras in the iPhone 14. One front camera for video calls and selfies, and two/three rear cameras for snapping photos of others, recording videos, scanning documents, and much other cool stuff. The rear cameras differ in their particular focal lengths and, as such, are given different names: Wide, Ultra Wide, and Telephoto.

Flash: You'll likely recognize the flash the very minute you see it. You can use it like a torch for illuminating your path while walking at night or searching for something in the dark. But far beyond this, you can use the flash to enhance the brightness and exposure of your pictures.

Microphone

Port: If you check the bottom of your phone, you'll see a port/hole. It's called a Lightning connector. It is where you'll insert your USB charger when you want to charge your phone or connect it to another device so that you can transfer data.

Note: There isn't any SIM tray, so you'll not have to worry about inserting a physical SIM card. Your iPhone uses an eSIM.

Customizing the iPhone 14 for Easy Access

Organize applications in folders on your device

To make it simpler to discover certain programs on your home screen pages, you may organize your apps into folders.

Creating folders

1. Hold down on the home screen's wallpaper until the apps start vibrating.
2. To create a folder, simply drag one program on top of a different app.
3. Drag more applications inside the folder.
4. The folder can include numerous app pages.
5. Tap then hold the folder to rename it, and then select Rename and a new name.
6. Retry if the applications begin to flicker by tapping the background image on the home screen.
7. When finished, press "Done" and then twice on the wallpaper on your home screen.

To remove a folder

1. Drag the entire app out of the folder after switching to it. The folder is automatically deleted.
2. Delete a folder and add an app to the home screen
3. Find the folder containing the app on the home screen page, then touch the folder to launch it.

4. Tap and hold down the application pending when it begins to vibrate.

5. From the folder, drag the application to the home screen.

CHAPTER 3: Getting Started with Your iPhone

Unboxing and Setting Up Your iPhone 14

Unboxing

The iPhone 14 comes in a tiny box, and inside the box is the phone, a USB-C to Lightning Cable, a SIM eject tool, and some documentation. You can use your old Apple 20W USB-C power adapter and AirPods or purchase these accessories separately if you don't have one.

Note: Power adapters, Airpods, and Apple Watches are sold separately. They don't come along with the phone.

How to Activate and Set up iPhone 14

In this article, we are going to lead you step-by-step over the procedure of configuring your iPhone 14 device and, if desired, transferring data from your previous device.

Step 1: Turn it on

We'll start with how to activate it. Push and hold the iPhone 14's side button until you see the Apple logo.

Step 2: Set It Up

The new startup screen appears, which is quite cool. Swipe up, then select your Language and Country. You should now ensure to see the Quick Start option.

If you wish to transfer data from your old iPhone, skip to step 4, where I've detailed everything. Tap Set Up Manually if you want to add it as a new device.

You'll need to be connected to the internet to activate your iPhone. Connect to Wi-Fi or use cellular data by inserting a SIM card.

The Data and Privacy option indicates that the device has been activated. You can now configure Face ID and create a Passcode.

Step 3: Restore Apps & Data

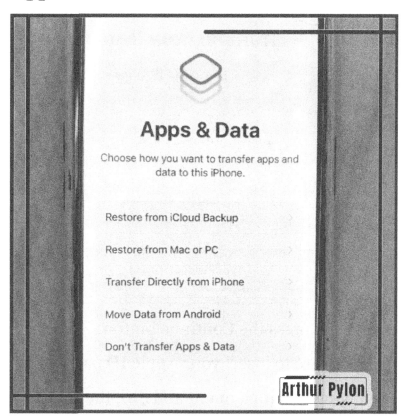

Following that, you'll see options to Restore our apps and data. I'll go with Don't Transfer App & Data. Sign in with your Apple ID now to use iCloud, or skip it if you'd rather do it later. Then, like the old devices, you can configure features such as automatic updates, Siri, screen time, and dark mode.

Step 4: Transfer Data from Old iPhone

The Home screen is displayed. If you wish to transfer data from your old iPhone, here's how to do it with Quick Start.

1. Keep your old device close to your iPhone 14.

2. To activate the quick start, toggle the screen off and on.

3. Continue by scanning the image on your new iPhone.

4. Continue with a few more setups until you reach the data transfer screen.

5. To begin transferring, press the Continue button.

6. When prompted, ensure to insert your Apple ID password.

7. After you've configured your payment and Siri, the transfer will begin.

Step 5: Data Transfer in Process

The amount of time it takes is determined by the size of the backup on the old device. The lock screen will appear a few seconds later. So, there you have it! Your settings and data have been moved to the new iPhone.

Creating an Apple ID and iCloud Account

Apple ID

Use a single Apple ID to access all Apple services. Only your complete name, date of birth, email address, and phone number are required.

Create An Apple ID When You Set Up Your Device

- Choose, "I forgot my password or I don't have an Apple ID."
- Tap, "Create an Apple ID for Free."
- Select, "your date of birth and provide your name." Click Next.
- Tap, "Use your existing email address" or "Get an iCloud email account for free."
- Follow the on-screen instructions when requested to validate your email address and enable two-factor authentication. If you want to skip this step, you will be requested to complete it later in Settings.

Create An Apple ID Using The App Store On Your Device

- Launch the App Store, then click the sign-in button.

- Select, "Create New Apple ID." When you aren't seeing this option, check to find out whether or not you have been logged off of your iCloud account.

- Follow the instructions on-screen. The provided email address will serve as your new Apple ID*

- Enter your billing and payment card details, then press Next. You may also choose, "**None**." Learn what to do if, "**None**" is shown or cannot be selected. You will not be charged unless you make a purchase.

- Verify your telephone number. This may assist validate your identity and, if necessary, regaining your account. Click Next.

- Locate the verification email received by Apple to your inbox and verify your email address.

- After verifying your email address, "you may use your Apple ID to sign in to the App Store, iTunes Store, and other Apple services like iCloud using your Apple ID."

Manage Apple ID Settings On iPhone

Your Apple ID gives you access to Apple services such as "App Store, iTunes Store, Apple Books, Apple Music, FaceTime, iCloud, and iMessage, among others."

Login With Your Apple ID

If you did not sign in through setup, perform these steps:

- Go to Configuration.

- Tap Log in to your iOS device.

- Enter your Apple ID credentials.

You may create an Apple ID if you do not already have one.

If you have enabled two-factor authentication to enhance the security of your account, please input the six-digit verification code when prompted. This code is typically sent to your trusted devices or the phone number linked with your Apple ID.

In case you cannot recall your Apple ID or password, you can visit the provided link to initiate the process of recovering your Apple ID. This will guide you through the necessary steps to regain access to your account.

Change Your Apple ID Configuration

1. Go to Configuration > [your name].

2. Perform any of the subsequent:

- Upgrade your contact details

- Modify your passphrase

- Add or delete Contacts for Account Recovery

- Manage and see your subscriptions

- Update your billing address and payment methods

- Share Family Resources

iCloud

iCloud saves your pictures, videos, documents, backups, and more securely and automatically syncs them across all your devices. You may also share photographs, calendars, notes, folders, and files with family and friends via iCloud. iCloud offers a free email account and 5 GB of storage space for your files. iCloud+ may be subscribed to for greater storage and other services.

Note: Some iCloud capabilities have minimal system requirements. Depending on the location or area, iCloud and its capabilities may or may not be accessible.

Modify Your iCloud Configuration

Sign in with your Apple ID, then complete the steps below:

1. To access iCloud, go to Settings > [your name] > iCloud.

2. Perform some of the subsequent:

3. See the status of your iCloud storage.

- Enable the desired options, including Photos, iCloud Drive, and iCloud Backup.

To learn how to adjust iCloud functions on your other devices, go here.

Ways To Use iCloud On iPhone

iCloud can automatically back up your iPhone.

Additionally, the following data may be saved in iCloud and synchronized across your iPhone and other Apple devices:

- Photos and movies;

- Files and documents;

- iCloud Mail

- Contacts, Calendars, Reminders, and Notes

- Information from third-party compatible applications and games

- Messages threads;

- Passwords and payment methods; see Make your passkeys and passwords accessible from any device with iPhone and iCloud Keychain

- Safari bookmarks and open tabs;

- Settings for News, Stocks, and Weather

- Home and Health records

- Voice memos

- Map favorites

Moreover, you may accomplish the following:

- Share photographs and videos.

- iCloud Drive enables file and folder sharing.

- Using Find My, you may find a lost device or share its position with friends and family. Consult Locate a device in Find My on iPhone and Locate a friend in Find My on iPhone for information on how to locate a device and a friend, respectively.

You may subscribe to iCloud+ for greater storage and access to iCloud Private Relay (beta), Hide My Email, and HomeKit Secure Video support.

Connecting to Wi-Fi and Cellular Networks

Connect to a Wi-Fi Network

1. Navigate to Settings.

2. Tap the **Wi-Fi** menu.

3. Click the switch next to **Wi-Fi** to green.

4. Then, click on the name of the Wi-Fi you wish to join.

5. Input the Wi-Fi password if prompted.

Using Personal Hotspot

To do this, move to Settings and choose Personal Hotspot. Meanwhile, choose Cellular if you fail to find it on the main settings page. From that page, you will find the option to set it up, which also requires contacting your carrier. Once you enter your Hotspot settings, enable it and choose how you need to connect it to other devices.

How to Set Up Personal Hotspot

Setting up your hotspot and sharing it with others around you guarantees you are sharing your internet connection with them. This method works when the other individual enables their Wi-Fi and connects to your device when you also enable your hotspot.

1. Set up your hotspot in the following ways:
2. Open Settings and choose Personal Hotspot.
3. Touch the slider close to "Allow Others to Join."
4. Then, adhere to the steps to create your hotspot password. (*NB:* The personal hotspot password and name are what other devices require before they will be allowed to connect and use your hotspot).

Change or set your Wi-Fi password:

1. To do this, open Settings.
2. Move down until you locate your Personal Hotspot.

Turn On Mobile Data

1. Navigate to Settings.
2. Click *Cellular*.
3. From here, click the switch next to *Cellular Data* to green.

Enable Smart Data Mode

If you don't need 5G data all the time, switching on Smart Data can conserve battery life and reduce your data consumption. Want to enable Smart Data? Here's how:

1. Navigate to Settings.

2. Now, tap "*Cellular*" to see the options menu.

3. From here, tap *"Cellular Data Options."*

4. At this point, tap "*Voice & Data*."

5. Finally, select "*5G Auto*" to turn on Smart Data mode.

Personalizing Your iPhone 14 Settings and Preferences

1. Customize Home Screen Layout:

- Long-press on your home screen to enter "Jiggle" mode.

- Drag app icons to various spots to rearrange them.

- To create app folders, drag one app icon onto another.

- Use the App Library feature to automatically organize apps into categories.

2. Set Wallpaper:

- Go to Settings > Wallpaper > Select a New Wallpaper.

- Select a wallpaper from the available options or choose your own photo.

- You may change the wallpaper on the lock screen and the home screen.

3. Adjust Display Settings:

- Go to Settings > Display & Brightness.

- Enable Dark Mode for a darker interface and reduced eye strain.

- Adjust the brightness level using the slider.

- Enable True Tone to adjust the display's color temperature based on ambient lighting.

4. Customize Control Center:

- Go to Settings > Control Center.
- Include or get rid of controls by tapping the "+" or "-" buttons.
- Reorder controls by dragging the handles on the right side.
- Include Accessibility Shortcuts for quick access to accessibility features.

5. Personalize Sounds and Haptics:

- Go to Settings > Sounds & Haptics.
- Customize ringtones, text tones, and vibrations for various notifications.
- Enable or disable system sounds, keyboard clicks, and lock sounds.

6. Configure Notification Settings:

- Go to Settings > Notifications.
- Customize notification settings for each app, including banners, alerts, sounds, and badges.
- Use "Focus" mode to control which notifications are allowed during specific activities.

7. Customize Siri Settings:

- Go to Settings > Siri & Search.
- Enable "Hey Siri" for hands-free activation.
- Customize voice feedback and language preferences.
- Manage Siri suggestions and app suggestions.

8. Personalize Privacy Settings:

- Go to Settings > Privacy.
- Review and manage app permissions for location, camera, microphone, contacts, and more.
- Enable or disable personalized ads and tracking.

9. Configure Keyboard Preferences:

- Go to Settings > General > Keyboard.
- Customize keyboard settings, including autocorrection, predictive text, and one-handed mode.
- Add and manage additional keyboards or language options.

CHAPTER 4: Communication Made Easy

Making and Receiving Phone Calls

Making a call on iPhone

Make and answer phone calls with your iPhone.

- To place a call using the Phone app 📞, enter the no. using the keypad, choose a contact from your contacts directory, or touch an earlier or preferred call. You may also choose someone from your favorites list.

Dial a number

You can dial the number you want to call with either 🎙 **Ask Siri** or the typical way.

🎙 **Ask Siri:** Say "dial" or "call," shadowed by a no. It would help if you spoke each digit separately (i.e., "three, one, two, six, six, four...").

Or the standard way:

1. From the Phone app's screen, tap **Keypad**.

2. The following options are available:

- **Use a different line:** On Dual sim models of iPhone (excluding iPhone 14 models in the US), touch the line at the top, then pick a different line to make the call.

- **Enter the number using the keypad**: Dial the number with your keypad, and if you made an error, touch ✕ to erase.

- **Redial the last number:** Tap 🔘 to view the last dialed number, then touch 🔘 a second time to call the number.

- **Paste a number you've copied:** Press and hold the phone number field above the keypad and click Paste.

- **Enter a 2-second (soft) pause:** Press and grasp the star (*) key till it changes to a comma.

- **Enter a hard pause (to pause dialing pending when you tap the Dial button)**: Press and grasp the pound (#) key till it changes to a semicolon.

- **Enter a "+" for international calls**: Press and grasp the "o" key till it changes to "+"

3. Click 🔘 to begin the call, and to end the call, touch 🔘.

Making a call from Favorites

1. From the Phone app's screen, touch **Favorites** (at the bottom left), then choose one of your Favorites to make a call. On Dual Sim devices, the iPhone picks the line for the call in the following order:

- The chosen line for this contact (i.e., if established).

- The line utilized to make (or answer) the last call to (or from) this contact.

- The default voice line.

2. Do any of the following to manage your Favorites list:

- **Add a favorite**: From **Favorites**, touch ┼, then select a contact to include to the Favorite list.

- **Delete or Rearrange favorites**: Click **Edit**.

Making a call from Contacts

You can make calls from your contacts list with either ⬤ **Ask Siri** or the typical way.

⬤ **Ask Siri:** Say something like, "Call Eve's mobile."

Or the standard way:

1. From the Phone app's screen, touch **Contacts**.

2. Select a contact and touch the number you wish to call.

N.B. When using a device that has a dual SIM card, the call will be placed through the standard route unless you have specifically designated a particular route for this contact.

Making a call from Recents

You can make calls from Recents with either ⬤ **Ask Siri** or the standard way.

⬤ **Ask Siri:** Say somewhat such as "Return my last call or Redial that last number."

Or the standard way:

1. From the Phone app's screen, touch **Recents**.

2. Touch the one you wish to call.

3. Touch ⓘ to get more details about a call and the caller.

N.B. A red badge specifies the number of missed calls from a contact.

Change your outgoing call settings

1. From your phone's **Settings** ⚙, touch **Phone**.

2. You have the subsequent options:

- **Turn on Show My Caller ID**: Your phone number can be shown in the "My Number" section. It is important to keep in mind that once someone contacts you using FaceTime, your contact information is going to be displayed irrespective of whether caller ID is switched off.

- **Turn on Dial Assist for international calls**: This feature enables your iPhone to automatically add the correct international or local prefix whenever you make a call.

Get in touch with your wireless provider if you want details regarding placing international calls, involving the rates which apply and any extra fees which might be incurred.

Answer or Decline incoming calls on your iPhone

Find out how to answer incoming calls on your iPhone, as well as how to hush them and reject them. Once you hang up on a call, the caller is sent straight to your voicemail. You could either send a text message in response or set a reminder to call them back.

Answer a call

Do any of the following to answer a call on your iPhone:

1. Touch
2. Drag the slider if your iPhone is locked

TIP: To have your iPhone declare the entire incoming calls or only the calls you receive whilst utilizing Bluetooth in your car or headphones, go to **Settings** , touch **Siri & Search** > **Announce calls,** and select an option. Siri recognizes the caller and allows you to accept the call by saying "yes" or decline it by saying "no."

Silence a call

To silence a call on your iPhone, press either volume button, the side button, or the Sleep/Wake button (based on your model).

N.B. After silencing a call, you can still answer it till the call goes to voicemail.

Decline a call

Choose any of the subsequent options to ignore an incoming call and have it sent straight to your voicemail:

1. Quickly double-press the side or Sleep/Wake button (depending on your model).

2. Click .

3. Or swipe up on the call banner to decline an incoming call

You may alternatively use the down arrow key on your keyboard for accessing these settings.

Do one of the following:

- Touch "Remind me" button, and then specify the time at which you would like to be reminded of returning the call.
- Touch **Message** and select a default reply or click **Custom** to write your reply.

To compose your standard replies, Go to **Settings** ⚙ and touch **Phone** > **Respond with text**, and click on any default message to swap it with yours.

N.B. In some nations or locations, when a call is turned down, the caller is immediately terminated rather than having sent to their voicemail.

Sending and Receiving Text Messages

Send and receive texts, photos, audio, and video messages with the Message app ✉. You can also use animated effects, Memoji stickers, iMessage apps, and Memoji stickers to personalize your messages.

Sending a message

For sending a text msg to a number of recipients, perform the subsequent steps:

1. At the top-right corner of your screen, touch  to start a new msg or click on a present msg.

2. Input the contact name, phone number, or Apple ID of all recipients, or you can touch ⊕ and select one or more contacts.

To send an SMS/MMS msg with a separate line on models with dual sim, touch the default line shown, then select the other one.

3. Touch the text field, write your text msg, and click ⬆ to send.

A green send button shows that the msg will be sent through SMS/MMS or your cellular service, while a blue send button means it will be delivered via iMessage.

If a msg cannot be delivered, an alert ⓘ appears. Touch the alert to resend the msg.

TIP: To find out the exact moment a msg was delivered or acquired, slide the bubble that contains the msg to the left.

Click on the name or phone number at the top of your screen to view conversation particulars. You can edit the contact card, view attachments, share your location, and lots more by tapping the contact. Scroll from the left edge or touch ⟨ to go back to the Messages list from a conversation.

Replying to a msg

Ask Siri. Say something like:

- "Reply, that's great news!"
- "Send a msg to Eve saying how about tomorrow."
- "Read my last msg from Matt."

TIP: Siri will read aloud any msgs that arrive on your device if you are using AirPods Pro, AirPods (2nd generation), or any compatible pair of earphones. You will then be able to react by saying the msg you wish Siri to deliver.

Or you can do the following:

1. On your Message list, touch the conversation you intend to answer to.

2. Touch the text field and compose your msg.

3. To deliver your msg, click ⬆.

TIP: Use a "Tapback" expression (e.g., a heart or a thumbs up) to quickly reply to a msg—double-touch on a msg bubble that you would like to reply to and choose a "Tapback."

Sharing your name and photo

When you create a fresh msg in "Messages" or reply to an existing one, you have the option of including both your name and a picture of yourself. Once you initially open "Messages" on your iPhone, you will need to adhere to the on-screen instructions to select a name and a profile picture for yourself. You may use a Memoji or create a bespoke picture using your photo.

1. Load up **Messages**, touch ⋯ , and then select **Edit Name and Picture**. From there, you can make every one of the subsequent changes, depending on whether you'd like to alter your name, picture, or sharing choices:

- **Change your name**: Click the text field where your name appears to edit it.
- Change your profile image: **Touch** Edit **and select an option.**
- **Turn sharing on or off**: Toggle the switch next to **Name and Photo Sharing** (green means it is on).
- **Change the people who can view your profile: Choose an option from the list below. Automatically share**. Note that **Name and Photo Sharing** must be turned on to use this feature.

N.B. You can also use your Messages name and photo for your Apple ID and My Card in Contacts.

Pin a conversation

Allow the people you contact most to come first by pinning precise conversations to the top of the Msgs list.

To pin a conversation, you either:

- Swipe right on a conversation and click 📌.
- Or, touch and grasp a conversation and drag it to the top of the Messages list.

Unpin a conversation

Remove individual discussions from their pinned position at the top of your Msgs list.

To unpin a conversation, you either:

- Touch and grasp a conversation and click ⚲.
- Alternately, you can touch and grasp a chat and then drag the msg to the bottom of your selection of Msgs.

Switching from a Message conversation to an audio call or FaceTime

You could start an audio call or FaceTime when chatting with a person in Messages.

- Click ▭◁ while in a messages conversation.
- Then touch FaceTime video or FaceTime audio.

Sending a msg to a business or group on iPhone

You can send audio messages, photos, and videos to groups of people with the Message app 💬. You can also use the business chat to send a msg to a business.

Replying to a specific msg in a group conversation

Replying to a particular msg within a group conversation enhances clarity and contributes to maintaining an organized discussion.

- Touch and grasp or double-touch a msg in a group conversation, then click

  .

- Then type in your response > .

Mentioning people in a group conversation

You could call other individuals attention to a specific msg in a group conversation by mentioning them. Regardless of whether they have the discussion muted, this function may nevertheless notify them of your msg if they have the appropriate parameters configured.

- Within a group conversation, start typing a contact's name in the text field.
- Touch the contact's name once it shows on your screen.

N.B. You could additionally reference a contact in a group conversation by typing "@" followed by the contact's name.

You can alter the notification settings for when you're cited in Messages. From **Settings** ⚙, touch **Messages** > **Notify Me**.

Changing a group name and photo

All the participants are included in the photo used in group conversations, which alters depending on who has been lately active. You are additionally given the chance to contribute an individual picture to the conversation that is taking place with the group.

- To modify the name or number of the group conversation, simply touch on the contact information displayed at the top, choose the option for **Change Name and Photo**, and then make your desired selection.

Using Business chat

You could communicate with companies who provide business chat through the Messages app. It gives you the ability to fix problems, find answers to inquiries, obtain recommendations for items to purchase, and other similar things.

1. Use Siri, Maps, Safari, or Search to find the business you want to chat with.

2. You can begin a conversation with the business by clicking the chat link in the search result. The chat link can appear in the form of the company logo, 💬 , or a text link.

N.B. Messages you send in Business Chat emerge in dark gray to differentiate them from messages sent utilizing SMS/MMS (in green) or iMessage (in blue).

Sending audios, photos, and video messages on your iPhone

You can send audios, photos, and video messages via the Messages app 💬 using SMS/MMS or iMessage service. You also have the option to save, share, or print attachments.

Sending an audio msg

1. To record an audio msg in a conversation, touch and grasp 🎙️ .

2. Touch ▶️ to playback the audio msg prior to sending it.

3. Touch 🔼 to send the audio msg or click ✖️ to cancel.

N.B. If you haven't selected to retain an audio msg, your iPhone will remove it in two mins once you've listened to it in order to free up storage space. To ensure that you always have access to your audio msgs, navigate to **Settings** ⚙️ , select **Messages** >

Expire (located underneath Audio Messages), and afterwards select **Never** from the drop-down menu.

Listening or replying to an audio msg

- To play an incoming audio msg, raise your iPhone to your ear.
- Raise it again to reply.

You can activate or deactivate this function by going to **Settings** ⚙, selecting **Messages**, and then either activating or deactivating the **Raise to Listen** setting.

Sending a photo or video

1. Whilst you are entering a msg, you have the option to do anything from the actions listed below:

- **Taking a photo within Messages**: Touch 📷, frame the shot in the viewfinder, and click ◯.

- **Taking a video within Messages**: Touch 📷, select a Video mode, and click ⬤.

- **Choosing an existing photo or video**: Click 🌸 to view recent shots, then swipe up to go through all Photos and albums.

52

2. Click  to send the msg or touch ⊗ to cancel.

Marking up or editing a photo

Before you send a photo in a Message conversation, you can mark up or edit the photo.

1. Click ✳ in the app drawer and pick a photo.

2. Touch the picture in the msg bubble and do one of the things below:

• Click **Markup**, then use the Markup tools to draw on the photo > **Save**.

• Click **Edit**, then use the photo editing tools to edit the photo > **Done**.

3. Click **Done** > **add a msg**, touch ⬆ to send the photo, or click ⊗ to erase the photo from the msg bubble.

Exploring Messaging Apps

iMessage

iMessage is Apple's built-in messaging service designed exclusively for iPhone users, enabling them to exchange text messages, photos, videos, and more with fellow iPhone, iPad, Mac, and Apple Watch users. Here are some essential features and useful tips to enhance your iMessage experience on your iPhone 14:

- Sending Messages with iMessage: iMessage utilizes an internet connection to transmit messages, eliminating the need for SMS charges. When sending a msg, if the recipient has iMessage enabled, it will be sent as an iMessage, indicated by the appearance of blue bubbles.

- Multimedia Messaging: iMessage supports the seamless sharing of photos, videos, documents, and various files directly within your conversations. To swiftly capture and send a photo or video, simply touch the camera icon, or utilize the "+" button to access other files stored on your device.

- Message Effects: Inject a touch of visual excitement into your messages using msg effects. While composing a msg, press and grasp the send button to access an array of effects such as balloons, confetti, fireworks, and more, adding an element of fun and surprise.

- Tapbacks: When you want to respond swiftly to a msg without typing out a full reply, take advantage of Tapbacks. By double-tapping a msg bubble, you could select from a diversity of reactions comprising thumbs up, heart, question mark, and others, allowing for quick and expressive responses.

- Stickers and Memojis: To enrich your conversations and express yourself creatively, iMessage provides a diverse collection of stickers and Memojis— customizable animated avatars. Access the App Store icon located next to the text input field to explore and use stickers and Memojis that resonate with your mood and personality.

Personalize iMessage Display Name:

- Open the Settings app on your iPhone.
- Scroll down and touch on "Messages."
- Touch on "Send & Receive."

- Select the appropriate display name or phone number under the "Start New Conversations From" section.**Enable or Disable Read Receipts:**

- Open the Settings app on your iPhone.

- Scroll down and touch on "Messages."

- Toggle the "Send Read Receipts" option to enable or disable it.

- When enabled, the sender will see a "Read" notification when you read their iMessage.

Customize iMessage Bubble and Screen Effects:

- Open the Messages app.

- Open a present conversation or initiate a new one.

- Touch and grasp the send button to access msg effects.

- Swipe left or right to select diverse bubble or screen effects.

- Touch the send button to apply the selected effect to your msg.

Use Emoji and Animoji in iMessage:

- Open the Mcssages app.

- Open a present conversation or initiate a new one.

- Touch on the App Store icon next to the text input field.

- Touch on the Emoji or Animoji icon to access the respective stickers.

- Browse and select the desired emoji or Animoji to send in your msg.

WeChat

WeChat is a famous messaging and social media app, particularly in China, with a wide range of features beyond just messaging. Here's an overview of using WeChat on your iPhone 14:

- Instant Messaging: WeChat allows you to send text, voice, and video messages to other WeChat users. You can start a conversation by touching the "+" icon in the top right corner then selecting "New Chat."

- Moments: WeChat's Moments feature is similar to a social media feed where you can share photos, videos, and posts with your friends. You can access Moments by touching the "Discover" tab at the bottom of the app.

- Voice and Video Calls: WeChat supports high-quality voice and video calls, allowing you to communicate with friends and family over the internet. You can initiate a call by selecting a contact and tapping the respective call button.

- WeChat Pay: WeChat Pay is an app-integrated digital payment service. It allows you to make payments, transfer money to friends, and even pay for goods and services at participating merchants.

- Mini Programs: WeChat Mini Programs are small applications within the WeChat app that offer various functionalities, such as games, shopping, travel, food delivery, and more. You can access Mini Programs by tapping the "Discover" tab and selecting "Mini Programs."

Personalize WhatsApp Profile:

- Open WhatsApp on your phone.
- Touch on the three-dot menu situated at the top right corner.
- Touch on "Settings" and then on "Profile."
- To modify your profile picture, simply touch on your current profile picture.
- Edit your name, status, and other profile details as desired.

Customize Chat Wallpaper:

- Open WhatsApp on your phone.
- Touch on the three-dot menu situated at the top right corner.
- Touch on "Settings" and then on "Chats."
- Touch on "Wallpaper" and select a wallpaper from the available options.
- Additionally, you have the option to choose a picture from your gallery or choose from a range of solid colors when changing your profile picture.

Enable or Disable Read Receipts:

- Open WhatsApp on your phone.
- Touch on the three-dot menu situated at the top right corner.
- Touch on "Settings" and then on "Account."
- Touch on "Privacy" and toggle the "Read Receipts" option to enable or disable it.
- When enabled, the sender will see two blue checkmarks when you read their msg.

Use Stickers and Emojis in WhatsApp:

- Open WhatsApp on your phone.
- Open a present chat or initiate a new one.
- Touch on the smiley icon next to the text input field.
- Browse through the available stickers and emojis.
- Touch on the desired sticker or emoji to send it in your msg.

Managing Contacts and Favorites

Use the Contacts app on your iPhone to store and manage your contacts. You can also synchronize with your private and business accounts (e.g., WhatsApp, Telegram, etc.).

Add and use contacts information

With the **Contacts** app , You may add, view, and modify contacts from your personal, business, and other accounts.

○**Ask Siri.** Say something like:

- "What is my sister's work address?"
- "Steven Carr is my brother."
- "Send a msg to my brother."

Create a contact

- From the **Contacts** app, touch +.

Note: Siri will additionally suggest fresh contacts to you depending on your activity across various apps, like the emails and invitations you get in Calendar and Mail, respectively. (To disable this feature, go to **Settings** > **Contacts** > **Siri & Search** after which press the toggle labeled **Enable Siri Recommendations for Contacts**.)

On the basis of how you use Contacts, Siri will also make recommendations for the contact data that you ought to utilize in different applications. (You may disable this option by going to **Settings** > **Contacts** > **Siri & Search**, then touching **Learn from this app**, and finally turning off the feature.)

Find a contact

Enter the contact information, like the name, phone, number, and address, on the search field at the top of your contacts list.

Share a contact

Touch a contact in your list of contacts, then touch the **Share Contact** button, and then select how you would like to distribute the contact details.

Quickly access a contact

Touch any of the choices that appear beneath the contact's name on the contact card to instantly send a msg, place a phone call or "FaceTime" call, write an email, or pay money using "Apple Pay. " These options are all conveniently located on the contact card.

To edit a contact's default phone number or email address, touch and grasp the phone number or email.

Delete a contact

- **Go to the** contact's card > Edit.
- Scroll down, then select **Delete Contact**.

Edit your contacts

With the Contacts app , you can add a birthday, change a label, allocate a picture to a contact, etc.

- Select a contact > **Edit**.
- Then these options are available:
- *Assign a photo to a contact*: Select **Add photo**, then capture a picture or include one from the Photos app.
- *Change a label*: Touch a label, then choose one in the list or create your own by tapping **Add Custom Label**.

- *Add a pronunciation*: Select **Edit**, scroll down, then select "**add field**." Touch a pronunciation name field, then type in how the contact's name should be pronounced. Siri will then pronounce their name using this pronunciation.
- Include a birthday, social profile, related name, etc.*: Touch ⊕ next to the option.*
- Permit calls or texts from contact(s) to override Do Not Disturb*: Select Ringtone **or** Text tone > Emergency Bypass.*
- *Add notes*: Touch the **Note field** to add notes.
- Include a prefix, phonetic name, pronunciation, and more*: Touch "add field" and choose an item in the list.*
- Remove contact information*: Touch ⊖ next to a field.*
- Once you are through, touch **Done.**

Add your contact info

Using the "Contacts" app ⊙, you are able to include your information on your contact card for that contact. Your Apple ID is used to generate your contact card, which is referred to as "My Card," on the iPhone; however, you might have to enter extra information (such as your name and address) to finish it.

Complete My Card

- Select **My Card** at the top of your contacts list > **Edit**. Contacts help you set up My Card by recommending addresses and phone numbers.
- Touch + the button and input your information if you were unable to identify "My Card," that should be near the top of the contacts list on your device. Touch on the name of yourself in the Contacts list after going to **Settings** ⊙ > **Contacts** > **My Info** on your device.

Edit My Card

- Click **My Card** at the top of your contacts list > **Edit**.

Create or edit your Medical ID

- Click **My Card** at the top of your contacts list > **Edit** > Scroll down, click **Create Medical ID,** or **Edit Medical ID.**

Use additional contact accounts

The Contacts app ⊚ permits you to include contacts from other accounts.

Use your Google contacts

- "**Go to** Settings ⊚ > Contacts > Accounts > Google**.**"
- "Sign in to your Google account, then turn on Contacts."

Use your iCloud account

- Open **Settings** ⊚ > {your name} > **iCloud** and turn on Contacts.

Add contacts from your other account

- "**Go to** Settings ⊚ > Contacts > Accounts > Add Account"
- "Select an account, sign in to the account and turn on Contacts."

Access a Microsoft Exchange Global Address List

- "**Go to** Settings ⊚ > Contacts > Accounts > Exchange**.**"
- " Log in to your Exchange account and enable Contacts."

Create a LDAP or CardDAV account to open business or school directories

- "**Open** Settings ⊚ > Contacts > Accounts > Add Account > Other**.**"
- Then select **Add LDAP Account** or **Add CardDAV** and enter the account information.

Keep contacts up to date across all your devices

You may utilize iCloud to ensure that every one of your Apple devices that are logged in with an identical Apple ID have the most recent version of your contact information and other facts.

- Touch **Settings** ⊚ > {your name} > **iCloud** and turn on Contacts.

Import contacts from a SIM card (GSM)

- **Go to** Settings ⊚ > Contacts > Import SIM Contacts**.**

Use Contacts from the Phone app

You can reach your contacts using the Phone app on your iPhone, and you can include previous callers to the Contacts app using that same app.

Adding a favorite

This allows you to put VIP contacts in your Favorites list for fast or instant dialing.

- From the **Phone app**, select a contact, then scroll down and select **Add to Favorites**.

Dial and save a number to Contacts

- From the **Phone app**, select **Keypad**, enter a number, then touch **Add Number**.
- **Pick either** Create New Contact **or** Add to Existing Contact.

Adding a recent caller to Contacts

- From the **Phone app**, click **Recents**, then click after the number.
- **Pick either** Create New Contact **or** Add to Existing Contact.

CHAPTER 5: Capturing and Managing Photos

Taking Photos and Using the Camera App

Mastering the camera app will help you capture stunning pictures and high-resolution photos that you can flaunt on the internet. This camera guide offers the important features to get you up and running with the Camera app in no time.

1. Access the Camera App via Control Center

2. Open the Control Center.

3. Click on the Camera tile to launch the app.

Switch Camera Modes

Once you launch the camera app, you can choose different camera modes. The camera mode for capturing images is different from that for shooting videos. For pictures, you have Pano, Photo, Portrait, etc., while for video, you have Slo-Mo, Time-Lapse, and Video.

Switching between the camera mode is easy. You can access the various camera modes in the horizontal scrolling menu at the app's bottom.

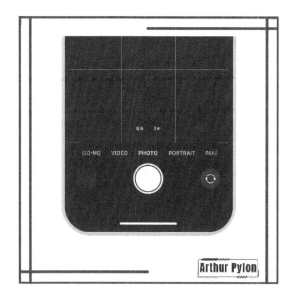

By default, it is set to Photo mode. You must swipe right to change to Video or another video mode, such as Slo-Mo.

Swipe left to revert to Photo or to select another photo mode.

Switch to the Front-Facing Camera

The front-facing camera lets you capture selfies without guessing too much, unlike the rear-facing camera. Switching from the rear-facing to the front-facing camera is easy. Regardless of the camera, you could additionally swipe left or right on the horizontal scrolling menu to choose your preferred camera mode.

To use the front camera, press the front-facing camera button (i.e., the camera icon with two split arrows heading in the same direction) in the lower right of the app.

Adjust Exposure

If you observe, you will see a yellow square lurking over your subject. Click on your subject on the display if you don't see it.

There is a sun icon next to the yellow square; you can use this to change the image's exposure, i.e., make the photo brighter or darker.

Click on the yellow sun icon to bring out the vertical slider.

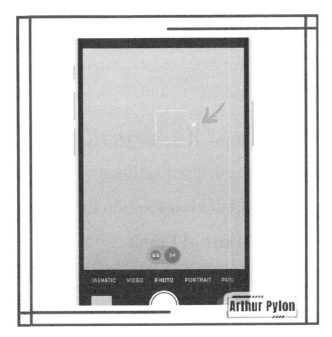

Increase the exposure by sliding up (brighter) or decrease it by sliding down (darker). Remove your fingers from there if you're okay with the lighting.

After choosing your subject and adjusting the exposure, you can decide to lock onto your subject so that even if you mistakenly toss your phone, your subject and exposure will remain the same. Hold down in the middle of the yellow square icon till the AE/AF Lock button appears on the display's top.

- AE = Auto Exposure
- AF = Auto Focus

Even after you've captured a photo, the AE/AF Lock will remain intact, allowing you to keep capturing photos at your desired settings.

Click anywhere within your field of view to undo the AE/AF Lock.

How to Use the Auto and Manual Flash

If you've taken a picture in a camera app before, you will observe that the camera sometimes uses the phone's flashlight to make the captured image look brighter. It also applies to the camera app on the iPhone. Auto Flash allows the camera to choose when to capture with a flashlight or do it manually.

1. If you need to adjust the Flash settings, click on the Flash (lightning bolt) button at the upper left.

2. To enable automatic flash, click **Auto**.

3. To enable your flash, click **On**.

4. To disable flash, click **Off**.

How to Use the Shutter Button

Once you are set to take a picture or video, you can do it by using your phone's volume key or the shutter button in the Camera app.

If you want to take a picture or record a video using the volume controls, start framing your shot/video and touch the volume up/volume down key to take the picture or record the video.

If you wish to take a photo with the shutter button, begin framing your image and tapping the large white circle at the bottom of the app.

Suppose you need to record a video, first frame it, and afterwards click the red icon at the bottom of the part. Following that, the circle will turn white. To stop the recording, click it again.

You can also take a Burst photo by pressing the shutter button. If you're wondering what the heck Burst photos are, read on. They are a series of photographs taken in rapid succession.

1. Long-press the shutter button to capture a burst image.

2. Hold the shutter button for a few seconds, then release your fingers.

3. Launch the Photos app to find your burst photo collection.

4. Choose the pictures you need to keep and delete the rest.

View the Captured Photo

To view the pictures you have taken using the camera app, you are going to have to close this application and then open the "Photos app" on your device. But wait, here's a tip: you can access the "Photos app" directly from the "Camera app." Click the small thumbnail at the lower left of the camera app to see your recently captured pictures and videos.

Take Live Photos

A Live Photo functions similarly to a GIF. It lets your camera shoot a few seconds of video and sound to produce a short clip of moving images. You can find the Live Photo button at the top of the camera screen.

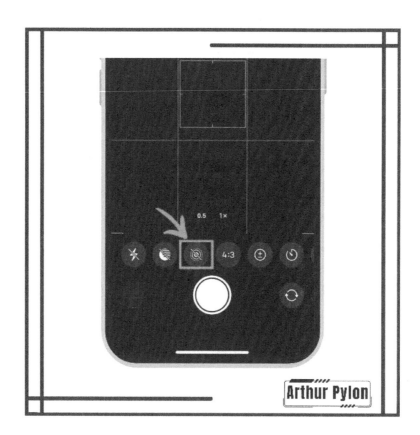

Edit your Pictures in Batch

The batch editing feature first appears in iOS 16. It allows users to customize a single image and then quickly apply those changes to an entire album's worth of photos. It means that changes made to one image can be easily copied and pasted into another or several images at once. It also implies that changes like brightness, shadows, and exposure will be copied and pasted onto the new photos.

How to Get Rid of Duplicate Photos

Unless you regularly filter the photos in your Photos app, they will likely contain duplicates. Having a lot of duplicates can be inconvenient when trying to sort through memories or find a specific picture.

Before iOS 16, removing duplicate photos from the Photos app was difficult. Duplicates in the Photos app are now easier to remove in iOS 16. If you don't want to delete duplicate photos, you can merge them. It ensures that no photos are lost while reducing the size of your photo library.

Record a Video

1. Navigate to Camera and swipe to select "*Video mode*."
2. Then, click the Record button. Otherwise, touch any of the volume keys to begin recording. There are a few things you can do while videoing.
3. Now, click the white Shutter icon to capture a still image.
4. Tweak the display to zoom in/out.
5. For further accurate zooming, long-press *1x*, and then push the slider towards the left.
6. Click the Record icon; otherwise, click any volume keys to end videoing.

You can adjust the frame rates and video resolution: Navigate to Settings and click on "*Camera*," then click "*Record Video*."

Record in Cinematic Mode

Cinematic mode lets you blur the background while keeping the subject sharp during a video.

1. Navigate to the camera and choose Cinematic mode.

2. Optional: Click **1x** before the shooting to zoom in.

3. To change the depth-of-field, click on the Depth Adjustment icon and then push the slider towards the left/right before shooting.

4. To begin recording, click the Record icon or press any volume controls.

5. A yellow frame on the interface indicates that the subject is in focus, whereas a gray frame indicates that the subject is recognized but not in focus. Click the gray button to adjust the focus; click again to keep the focus on the subject steady.

6. If no one appears in the video, click somewhere on the screen to make it the main focus.

7. Long-press the display to lock the focus at a particular distance.

8. Click the Record icon to end the shoot.

Record a Slow-Motion Video

A video in slow-mo mode will record as usual, but you can only see the slow-motion effect anytime you play it back.

1. Navigate to the camera and swipe to Slo-mo mode. Or, click the Camera Back-Facing icon to shoot Slo-mo videos using the front camera.

2. Click on the Record icon to begin videoing.

3. If needed, click the Shutter icon to capture a still image while videoing.

4. Click the Record icon again to end the recording.

By clicking on the video thumbnail and selecting "**Edit**," you will be able to play back a portion of the video at a slower pace whilst allowing the remaining portion to play at its regular speed. You may mark the part of the video that you want to play back in slow motion by dragging the vertical bars that are located beneath the viewer.

To adjust the slo-mo mode frame rate and resolution: Navigate to Settings and choose "*Camera*." Then click on "*Record Slo-mo*."

Change the Camera's Focus and Exposure

The iPhone's camera automatically locks the focus and exposure, but if you need to do it manually, here's what to do:

1. Navigate to Camera.
2. Click on display to display the automatic focus section and exposure setting.
3. Now, click on where you wish to pin the focus area.
4. Slide the Adjust Exposure icon ☀ next to the focus section up or down to change the exposure.
5. To steady the manual focus and exposure settings for future recordings, long-press the focus section till the *AE/AF Lock* button shows up; click the display to unlock settings.
6. You can accurately configure and stabilize the exposure for future recordings. Click the ◉ Camera Controls icon and the ⊕ Exposure button. Now, drag the slider to change the exposure. The exposure will remain that way for subsequent shots. You can still save it, so it doesn't reset when you launch the Camera app. Navigate to Settings, click the Camera option, and then choose "*Preserve Settings*." Now, toggle on "*Exposure Adjustment*."

Enable/Disable the Camera's Flash

The camera app will automatically turn on the flash when you take a picture that needs more illumination. You can manually set the flash before taking a photo. Here's how:

1. Click on the ⚡ Flash button to activate or deactivate the automatic flash. Click on the ⌄ Camera Controls icon, and then click the Flash icon under the frame to select On, Off, or Auto.

Capture a Photo with a Filter

Filters are tools used to add color effects to photos, and you can use them on the camera app to give your photo a stunning look.

1. Navigate to Camera.

2. Swipe to Photo or Portrait mode.

3. Now, click on the ⌄ Camera Controls icon.

4. Click the ⦿ Filters icon.

5. Swipe left or right under the viewer to see a preview of the filters, and click one to use it.

Use the Timer

The camera app has a timer button that you can touch to give you more time before the shot is taken.

1. To configure the timer, navigate to Camera.

2. Click on the ⌄ Camera Controls icon and ⏱ Timer icon.

3. Now, select *3s* or *10s*.

4. Afterward, hit the Shutter icon to start the timer.

Use Grid to Straighten Your Photos

Adding a grid to the camera interface can assist you in straightening and adjust your shot.

1. Select the "Settings" application.

2. Select "Camera."

3. Now, select "Grid."

4. After you've taken a photo, use the editing tools in the "Photos app" to fine-tune it and change the horizontal and vertical orientation.

Take Macro Photographs and Videos

The ultra-wide camera can take macro photos and videos.

1. Navigate to the camera and go 2cm closer to the subject to allow the camera to lock in focus automatically.

Enable/Disable HDR Video

1. Navigate to Settings.

2. Click on "*Camera*."

3. Now, click "*Record Video*."

4. Toggle on or off "*HDR Video*."

5. Take Burst Mode Shots

6. Burst mode lets you take a shot of a moving subject or multiple high-speed pictures at once, so you can have different images to pick from.

Editing and Enhancing Photos on the iPhone

1. Open the Photos app on your iOS device.

2. Browse through your photo library and select the photo you want to edit. You can touch on the "Photos" tab at the bottom to access your entire photo collection or use the search bar to find a precise photo.

3. Once you have selected the photo, touch on the "Edit" button situated at the top right corner of the screen. This will open the editing interface.

4. In the editing interface, you will find various editing tools and options at the bottom of the screen. These tools include cropping, adjusting exposure, color adjustments, filters, and more.

5. To make adjustments, touch on the desired tool and use the sliders or controls provided to modify the photo. For example, you can drag the exposure slider to

brighten or darken the image, adjust the saturation for more vibrant colors, or apply a filter to change the overall look.

6. As you make changes, the photo preview will update in real-time, allowing you to see the effect of your edits. You can experiment with different adjustments till you achieve the desired result.

7. Once you are satisfied with the edits, touch on the "Done" button at the bottom right corner of your screen to save the changes. In your picture library, the altered photo will replace the original.

Organizing and Sharing Photos in the Photos App

1. Launch the Photos application on your iOS device.

2. Accessing your photo albums is as simple as tapping on the "Albums" tab located at the bottom of your screen. Here, you'll find pre-existing albums like "Camera Roll," "Favorites," and "Recently Deleted." Additionally, you can create new albums by tapping the "+" icon.

3. Creating a new album is a breeze. Just touch on the "+" icon, enter a name for the album, and select the desired photos by tapping on them. To save the album, touch on the "Done" button.

4. To include images to an established album, navigate to the album and touch on the "+" icon. Then, choose the photos you wish to include and touch the "Done" button to confirm your selection.

5. Sharing a photo is effortless. Open the photo you want to share and touch on the share icon, represented by a square with an upward-pointing arrow. From there, select your preferred sharing method, such as Messages, Mail, or popular social media platforms like Facebook or Instagram.

Using iCloud Photos for Backup and Sync

1. Go to your iPhone's Settings app.

2. To see the options associated with your Apple ID, touch on your name at the very top of the settings screen.

3. Select "iCloud" from the list of options.

4. Scroll down and touch on "Photos."

5. To activate the function, turn on the "iCloud Photos" option. This will automatically back up your photos to iCloud and sync them across your Apple devices.

6. If you want to optimize your iPhone's storage, you can enable the "Optimize iPhone Storage" option. Lower-resolution copies of your images will be kept on your device, while full-resolution ones will be stored in iCloud.

7. Additionally, you can choose to enable the "Upload to My Photo Stream" option if you want to sync your most recent photos across your devices without using iCloud storage.

CHAPTER 6: Useful Apps and Tools for Seniors

As technology continues to advance, smartphones have become indispensable our daily lives, including for seniors. The iPhone 14, being the latest iteration of Apple's popular smartphone, offers a range of useful features and applications that can greatly benefit seniors. These essential apps can help enhance communication, health monitoring, entertainment, and more.

Health and Fitness Apps for Staying Active

Investing in your health via your iPhone won't cost you anything more than your monthly mobile data plan if you use the proper applications. While the iPhone has a comprehensive health app, it still lacks several features that are essential for ensuring your own well-being.

In this section, we'll take a look at some of the top iPhone applications in the field of health. You may take a basic step toward controlling your health and wellbeing by using one of these apps.

It is important to note that our discussion does not suggest these apps should replace the guidance of a qualified medical practitioner.

Glucose Buddy Diabetes Checker - Selected by Editors

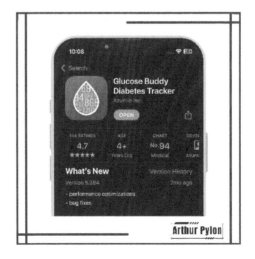

Diabetes is fatal in its most extreme forms. However, your chances of discovering diabetes early and preventing its complications are greatly improved if you start checking your blood glucose level sooner rather than later. Glucose Buddy may assist you in controlling your blood sugar regardless of your prior experience with diabetes. Feel free to include it into your current therapy plan, whether it's for yourself or a loved one. The heart rate monitor is functional in both standing and sitting positions, allowing you to track your cardiovascular fitness in any environment. The app can also communicate with a Bluetooth glucose meter. A quick inquiry about your history with diabetes will be shown when you first launch Glucose Buddy. After then, it's up to you to set your own goals.

It's also possible to link it with Apple's Health app. When connected to the Health app, it may record how far you walk each day. So, before you use this sync choice, you might want to set up walking stability on your iPhone. A subscription grants you access to the app, with increasing benefits at higher levels. For seven days, you may try out the service without taking any chances to determine whether it meets your needs.

MyFitnessPal: Calorie Counter is the best fitness health application

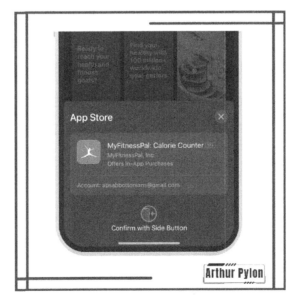

I recommend MyFitnessPal if you want to lose weight and cut back on your daily donut intake. This is accomplished through deliberate reinforcement, a fast daily step program, and consistent physical exercise.

MyFitnessPal is a useful tool for monitoring your calorie intake, physical activity levels, and progress toward your weight loss objectives.

The meal planner can be used to save dishes for later use. My favorite function is being able to scan the barcode of a dish to get the calories and other information about it.

The app also includes a database of meal combinations, so you can research a dish you're interested in including in your diet and get an idea of how many calories it contains.

When you set a calorie deficit, MyFitnessPal will deduct the calories from your daily calorie allowance to account for the new foods you've added.

As a result, you can try to find a happy medium where you aren't taking any fewer or more risks than necessary.

When you combine strategic meal planning with consistent and challenging exercise, you can more easily shed unwanted pounds and keep them off.

Not only does this app aid in meal preparation, but it also supplies you with scheduled workouts to help you meet your fitness goals. The dashboard displays time-based data, allowing you to track your overall progress toward your objectives.

Instant Heart Rate: HR Monitor - Top heart health application

Your irregular heartbeat may be a warning sign of cardiovascular illness that you have been ignoring. Instant Heart Rate Monitor is a simple tool for monitoring your heart rate in BPM (BPM).

The app does this by taking a reading of your heart rate from your index finger via the iPhone's camera. Up till the timer goes off, maintain finger placement over the camera's lens. A comment feature for results is also helpful for tracking progress.

The premium plan gives you access to further insights into the health information indicated by your heart rate, in addition to assessing your stress levels and presenting you with a heart report.

The daily reminder is provided for those who have a habit of forgetting their daily routine.

By marking the time at which a measurement is taken, you may get insight into the cumulative effect of your daily habits on your cardiovascular wellness over time. When choosing Post-exercise, for instance, you may be able to specify that the heart rate reading was recorded after you finished your workout.

Additionally, you may see past statistics in the app's Insights area. Do you plan to share your results with others? The answer might be as close as the tip of your finger.

If you utilize the iPhone's built-in Health app, you may connect Heart Rate Monitor with it for even more convenient health data sharing.

WebMD: Symptom Checker - Best for Doctors

In spite of WebMD's usefulness for a wide range of medical concerns, its symptom checker particularly stands out. It's essential to note that despite the software's popularity, it is not meant to replace actual medical treatment. If you often forget to take your prescription, the app might serve as a reminder to do so.

WebMD also has a useful drug interaction function that notifies users if they are taking several prescriptions at once, which might raise the likelihood of adverse reactions. Questioning the efficacy of a prescribed drug? The pill's lot number may be used to trace its history.

You may use the pill identifier to look up information on a pill by typing in its name or looking for a picture of it. In the event that you have no idea what you are doing in the medical area, you shouldn't use this software.

WebMD's symptom checker lets you touch anywhere on a human image or enter specific keywords to get information about your condition. Consequently, the app's aggregation of current health news items and how-to tutorials is helpful for expanding your understanding.

Strava: Run, Ride, Hike - Best motion workout app

If you use Strava, you're certain to work up a sweat every time. Whereas most applications just provide a list of recommended workouts and routines, Strava taps into the collective intellect of its users to help you achieve your objective. As a result, the app may sync with your Facebook and phone's contact list to facilitate meeting individuals in your region who share your interests.

Strava may be used for any fitness-related activity you want to track. It contains a built-in trail map so you can locate new places to walk, ride, or jog for additional pleasure and fitness.

As was noted previously, Strava's attractiveness depends on how effectively it combines with users' other social activities. As a consequence, the application enables users to establish teams and construct group challenges, such as those in which they work toward shared objectives and honor their top performers.

You can avoid losing money or wasting time by keeping track of your distance using the app's built-in GPS tracker.

Productivity and Organization Apps

Notes App

There are many different note-taking apps available for iPhone users, but the Notes app is a great option if you want a simple, straightforward way to take and manage notes.

Step 1: To create a new note, open the app then touch on the "+" icon in the top-right corner of your screen; This will bring up a blank page where you can start typing out your thoughts or ideas.

Step 2: To edit an existing note, simply touch on it from within your list of notes and make any changes that you need to. When you're finished editing, just touch on "**Done**" in the top-right corner of the screen.

Step 3: To delete a note, swipe left on it from within your list of notes and then touch on "**Delete.**

Step 4: Adding Images & Attachments: With the Notes app, you can effortlessly include images and attachments in your notes. This feature simplifies the process of enhancing your notes by adding visual elements and additional files.

To do this, simply touch on the "**Aa**" icon in the top-left corner of the screen and select either "**Insert Photo or Video**" or "**Attach File**" from the menu that appears.

Step 5: Organizing Your Notes: Once you have created several notes, you may want to organize them into different folders so they are easier to find later on.

To do this, touch on the "**Folders**" icon in the navigation bar at the bottom of your screen and then select or create a new folder as desired.

Calculator App

The Calculator app on the iPhone 14 is a versatile tool that assists you in various tasks. Whether you need to calculate a tip at a restaurant or perform complex calculations for work, the app is equipped to handle it all.

Step 1: Just slide up from the bottom of your screen to activate the **Control Center**, then press on the **Calculator** symbol to launch the calculator application on your device.

Step 2: The first thing you'll find is that there are two different modes - **Standard and Scientific**- which can be accessed by tapping on the Mode button in your top left corner.

- The standard mode is great for basic arithmetic, while the Scientific mode offers more advanced features like trigonometric functions and logarithms.

No matter which mode you're in, using the calculator is pretty straightforward - just enter numbers and operators like +,-,/,* into the keypad and hit '=' when you're done to see your result.

One neat trick worth knowing is that if you make an error whilst inputting numbers or operators, simply shake your iPhone 14 to clear everything and start over again!

Whether you're solving simple math problems or complex equations, this handy tool will help get the job done quickly and easily."

Calendar App

The Calendar app on the iPhone 14 provides an excellent means to stay organized and stay on top of your schedule. It allows you to seamlessly add events, set reminders for important tasks, and even share your calendar with others for better coordination and collaboration.

The app also syncs with other calendar apps, so you can always stay up-to-date.

- To get started using the Calendar app, simply open it and start adding events. You can create a new event by tapping on the **"+"** button in the top right corner.
- Then, fill in all the necessary information, such as the title, location, date, and time. Once you're done, touch "**Save**" to add it to your calendar.
- If you wish to set a reminder for an event, touch on it and then select "**Add Reminder**."

From there, choose when you want to be reminded and whether or not you want an alert sound or badge icon displayed when the reminder goes off.

- Touch "**Done**" when you're finished setting up your reminder.
- To share your calendar with others, navigate to the Settings menu and locate the "**Shared Calendars**" option. From there, you can invite individuals by sending them an email invitation or entering their iCloud address if they utilize that service

When they accept your invitation, their name will appear under Shared Calendars in settings.

Clock App

The iPhone 14 comes with a pre-installed Clock app that can be used to set alarms and timers and view the time in different time zones.

The app is user-friendly and offers a multitude of features that can greatly benefit its users.

- Alarms can be customized with different sounds and settings, making it easy to wake up in the morning or remind yourself of an upcoming event.

- Timers can also be set for specific tasks or activities, allowing you to keep track of how long you have been working on something or how long till your next break.

- The world clock feature is perfect for those who often travel or need to stay aware of what time it is in multiple places at once.

Overall, the Clock app on the iPhone 14 is a helpful tool that can make life easier by keeping track of important times and events.

- To set the alarm, open the **Clock app** and touch on the "**Alarm**" tab.

- Locate and touch the "+" button situated in the top-right corner of the screen.

- In the alarm creation screen, you can choose the specific time or day when you want the alarm to activate.

- Customize the alarm by selecting the preferred sound for it to play.

- Additionally, you have the option to configure whether or not the alarm should repeat.

- Once you have everything configured how you like it, simply touch "**Save**" in the top-right corner.

To track time with a timer or stopwatch, open the Clock app and touch on either the "**Timer**" or "**Stopwatch**" tab. With timers, you can set how long they should run before going off.

Entertainment and Media Streaming Apps

Music Apps

No pressure to make a purchase, at all. To avoid this, I recommend signing up for a monthly music streaming service like Apple Music, Spotify, or Amazon Prime Music. Every music fan should get these free iPhone music applications. Some of these apps require a subscription fee in order to use them, but the vast majority can be accessed without spending a dime. Nonetheless, half of them are zero cost because of commercials.

Download the app(s) of your choice, pair your iPhone with a Bluetooth speaker, and listen away. It's easy to utilize a speaker in the shower while keeping the windows closed.

- **Spotify**

Spotify is the most commonly used music streaming service since it has more users than any of its competitors. There's a ton of songs to choose from, great tools for teamwork and socializing, and radio stations in the vein of Pandora. With the introduction of podcasts, Spotify is expanding beyond its original purpose as a music streaming service. These programs aren't available anywhere else.

You may now listen to an unlimited number of songs and playlists for no cost (but an account is still required). In the past, a monthly subscription to Spotify on an iOS device cost $10.

The commercial breaks are a part of this version. All of Spotify's features are available for a monthly price of $10.

By subscribing at this level, you have access to a higher quality audio stream, uninterrupted playback, and the ability to download songs for offline listening.

- **Apple Music**

On every iPhone, you'll find the Music app. The easiest way to learn about Apple Music is to actually use it.

Apple Music gives you access to almost the entire iTunes Store on your PC and iPhone for only $10 per month ($15 for households with up to six members). If you don't need access to features like lossless audio, lyrics, and music videos, you may sign up for the $5/month Voice Plan instead. You may try out the service without any commitment for 30 days. The service allows users to save songs for later listening, make and share playlists, and follow the careers of their favorite artists.

Beats 1 radio is included in the show's radio segment. Some of the world's most well-known DJs, musicians, and music tastemakers choose the playlists for Beats 1, a 24-hour radio feed broadcast throughout the globe. Radio not only has Beats 1 but also a tailored music streaming service that is quite similar to Pandora.

Apple Music is a universal streaming service, meaning it works on every mobile device and has every feature imaginable.

- **Amazon Music**

Most people have heard of Amazon Prime, but only a fraction of those same individuals will have heard of Amazon Music. Prime users may access a number of exclusive features in the Amazon Music app.

More than two million songs, playlists, and radio stations may be streamed instantly via Amazon Prime Music. The program is completely commercial-free and may be accessed by anybody with an Amazon Prime membership. We also offer a family plan that covers up to six people.

You may download, save on your computer, or have delivered to your house any music you buy from Amazon, whether it be for streaming, MP3 listening, or physical delivery.

With an Amazon Music Unlimited membership, you get access to a comprehensive music streaming service. With a monthly subscription of $9.99 ($7.99 for Prime members), you may listen to millions of songs, playlists, and radio stations. It also has the ability to save music locally for playback when there is no network connection.

In the Amazon Music app, Alexa is available at no extra cost. The app includes Amazon's Alexa, the voice-activated digital assistant that runs the Echo line of devices, bringing all of Alexa's features and capabilities to your mobile device.

- **YouTube Music**

YouTube has become one of the most popular online music listening destinations, despite being more often associated with video. Listen to some of the numerous available tracks or even whole albums online. Billboard chart placements of individual songs and videos are influenced by how well these recordings and snippets perform.

Start with a video or song on YouTube Music, and the service will provide station and playlist suggestions based on your first selection. Much like the other applications we've recommended, Stations uses your listening history to create personalized playlists. To avoid commercials, save videos and music for offline viewing, and play music even while your phone is locked, you may subscribe to YouTube Premium for $12.99 per month.

Movies Applications

Watching a movie on an iOS device like an iPhone 14 is one of the best ways to unwind and relax. Right? The movie app on the iPhone is a hidden bonus, a great method to combat boredom since it delivers a totally absorbing pastime. There are a ton of applications like this out there, but only the best ones can elevate your iPhone movie-watching experience to the next level.

- **Netflix**

Netflix, the leader in the streaming video business, has the most downloaded movie app for the iPhone. If you own an iPhone, Netflix is the only movie app you'll ever need. Online video content delivery based on membership.

In-Depth Looks:

- Take a look at the various sections to find the top films in a wide range of genres.
- A Lookup Box Create a top-ten list of your favorite TV series and movies.
- If you use the "Recently Seen" feature, you can take up your movie viewing where you left off.
- The iPhone 6 and 7 are capable of streaming in 1080p.
- Observe films that are dubbed

- iOS 9 and later versions provide a plethora of games that can be downloaded from the App Store.

- **iTunes**

Apple iTunes is perhaps the best media player available, capable of playing almost every kind of media file, including movies, music, and podcasts. When it comes to transferring videos to an iPhone, iTunes is the go-to program. For those who own an iPhone and an Apple ID, this is the store from which they may get media.

- **Amazon Prime Video**

Netflix is the primary streaming service that closely rivals Amazon Prime Video. This highly recommended iPhone movie app offers a plethora of options, surpassing even Netflix in terms of variety. Notably, it is an excellent choice for young users. In terms of technological advancements, Amazon Prime takes the lead over Netflix. Being the pioneer consumer service, it was the first to provide ultra HD streaming and high dynamic range (HDR) content at no additional charge.

Social apps

These are the official iPhone and iPad applications for some of the most famous social networking sites, and they're available for no cost. We've selected the top social networking applications for the iPhone and iPad from the many that are currently available on the App Store.

- **Facebook**

The official Facebook app is essential because of the social connections it facilitates. In Apple's ecosystem, this is the official Facebook app. If you're looking for a popular and user-friendly social networking site, go no further than Facebook.

With Facebook for iOS, you can use your iPhone or iPad to stay abreast of what your friends are up to, check out and share images and videos, play games, download and install applications, and get quick response from loved ones who like or comment on your posts through push notifications.

- **Twitter**

Twitter, a social networking software that can be used on the iPhone, iPad, and Apple Watch, is fantastic for keeping up with the news. This social network app lets you stay abreast of happenings in the political, sporting, and entertainment realms, as well as participate in discussions about these events, and have access to special features like films, live broadcasts, and recollections. It is now possible to post videos, photos, stickers, and events to Twitter from an iOS device such the iPhone, iPad, or Apple Watch.

- **Instagram**

When using an iOS device, Instagram makes it simple to include various images, videos, and text in your story. You may now utilize Instagram, one of the most downloaded social networking applications. To transmit photographs, videos, messages, and feed items that vanish after being seen, use this app. There's a bar at the top of your screen where you may view stories and live videos from the people you follow.

CHAPTER 7: Accessibility Features for Enhanced Usability

Overview of iPhone's Accessibility Options

Most people know that their iPhone has various accessibility settings that can be adjusted to suit their needs. However, many are not aware of the full extent of what these settings can do.

The first thing to note is that these accessibility features can be found in the **Settings** app under "**Accessibility.**"

- One feature that may be particularly useful for some users is **VoiceOver**. This feature provides spoken descriptions of what is happening on your screen, which can be helpful if you are blind or have low vision.

- Another useful setting is **Zoom**, which allows you to magnify your screen, so it's easier to see. There are also options for adjusting font size and color filters.

- If you have difficulty using your hands, a few options are available to make your iPhone more accessible.

- One option is **AssistiveTouch**, which adds a virtual home button to your screen, so you don't have to press the physical button.

- There's also an option called **Switch Control**, which lets you use switches or other input devices instead of touching the screen directly.

- You can enable **Display Accommodations** to make text and images easier to see if you have trouble seeing the screen.

- There are also options to **increase contrast and reduce motion.**

- If you need help hearing what's happening around you, try enabling **Live Listen** in the **Hearing section** of **Settings**; This will use your iPhone's microphone to amplify sounds so you can better hear them.
- For those with hearing **impairments**, several options, such as closed captioning and subtitles, can be turned on to make videos more accessible.

Enabling and Customizing VoiceOver and Zoom

VoiceOver and Zoom are accessibility features on the iPhone 14 that assist users with visual impairments or who require larger text and interface elements. Here's how you can enable and customize VoiceOver and Zoom on your iPhone 14:

Enabling VoiceOver:

1. Open the Settings app.
2. Touch "Accessibility" and then select "VoiceOver."
3. Toggle the VoiceOver switch to the "On" position.
4. A confirmation dialog will be displayed, notifying you that enabling VoiceOver will modify the gestures used to control your device. Touch on "Enable" to proceed.
5. VoiceOver is now enabled, and your device will read aloud items on the screen as you interact with them.

Customizing VoiceOver:

1. In the VoiceOver settings, you can adjust the speaking rate, which controls how quickly VoiceOver speaks.
2. You can also customize the voice used by tapping on "Speech" and selecting a different voice or adjusting the speaking rate.
3. Additionally, you can adjust other settings like VoiceOver gestures, audio ducking, and verbosity to tailor the experience to your preferences.

Enabling Zoom:

1. Open the Settings app.

2. Touch "Accessibility" and then select "Zoom."

3. Toggle the Zoom switch to the "On" position.

4. You can choose between different Zoom options like "Zoom Region" and "Zoom Filter" to customize the zoomed view.

Customizing Zoom:

1. In the Zoom settings, you can adjust the Zoom region to control which part of the screen is magnified.

2. You can choose between "Full Screen Zoom" or "Window Zoom" depending on your preference.

3. You can also enable or disable "Follow Focus," which automatically moves the zoom window as you interact with the screen.

4. Adjust the maximum zoom level using the "Zoom Filter" option to control the level of magnification.

5. Additionally, you can enable "Show Controller" to display a control panel for zooming in and out.

Using VoiceOver and Zoom:

1. With VoiceOver enabled, you can navigate your iPhone 14 by using a combination of gestures, such as tapping, swiping, and using two or three fingers.

2. VoiceOver will read aloud the items on the screen as you interact with them.

3. When Zoom is enabled, you can zoom in and out by double-touching the screen with three fingers. You can also use the Zoom controller to regulate the zoom level.

Using Siri for Voice Control and Assistance

Siri is a clever virtual assistant unique and exclusive to the iPhone models. Talking to Siri is an easy and super-fast way of getting things done. You can ask Siri to set a timer, report on the weather, translate a phrase, find a location, etc. Siri adapts to you, therefore, the longer you utilize Siri, more accurately it will understand your requirements.

N.B. It is required that your iPhone have access to the internet in order to utilize Siri (cellular data fees might be charged).

Getting started with Siri

After you initially turn on your iPhone, you will have the opportunity to configure Siri.

In the event that you did not, nonetheless, navigate to **Settings** ⚙ > **Siri & Search** and perform any of the subsequent actions:

- If you prefer summoning Siri with your voice: Turn on **Listen for "Hey Siri."**

- If you want to activate Siri by pressing a button, you may either turn on the option to **Press Side Button** for Siri (on iPhone models with Face ID) or switch on the option to **Press Home for Siri** (on iPhone models with a Home button).

Summoning Siri with your voice

Siri responds out loud when you summon Siri with your voice.

1. To summon Siri, say "Hey Siri," then instruct Siri to perform a task for you or ask a question. For instance, say something like, "Hey Siri, set an alarm for 5 a.m." or "Hey Siri, what is today's weather report?"

2. If you want to instruct Siri to execute another task or answer another question, say "Hey, Siri" again or click .

N.B. If you want to stop Siri from replying to "Hey Siri," put your device face down, or from **Settings** ⚙, touch "**Siri & Search**" and turn off **Listen for** "**Hey Siri.**"

Summoning Siri with a button

When your iPhone is in ring mode, Siri responds aloud when you call for Siri with a button. And when iPhone is in silent mode, Siri responds silently.

1. Based on your iPhone model, do either of the things as follows:

- **iPhone models with Face ID**: Press and grasp the side button.

- **iPhone models with Home button**: Press and grasp the Home button.

2. When Siri appears, instruct Siri to perform a task or ask Siri a question.

3. If you want to instruct Siri to perform another task or answer another question, say "Hey, Siri" again or click .

Correcting your request if Siri misunderstands you

- **Rephrase your request**: Click ⬤ and say your request differently.

- **Spell out part of your request**: Click ⬤ and repeat your request by spelling out the words that Siri misunderstands. For instance, say, "Send a msg to," then spell the person's name.

- Changing your msg prior to sending it**: Say, "Change it."**

- **Use text to edit your request**: You can edit your request if you see it onscreen. Touch the request, then edit it with the onscreen keyboard.

- Use type as an alternative of speaking to Siri

You can type in your request instead of saying it.

- **From** Settings ⬤, **touch** Accessibility > Siri**, then enable** Type to Siri**.**

- To make a request, summon Siri and type in what you want Siri to do for you.

Tips for Enhancing Visual and Hearing Accessibility

Tips for Enhancing Visual Accessibility:

Increase Text Size:

- Adjust the text size on your device to make it easier to read. Go to Settings > Display & Brightness > Text Size and drag the slider to increase the text size.

Bold Text:

- Enable the Bold Text option in Settings > Display & Brightness to make the text more prominent and easier to read.

Dynamic Text:

- Use the Dynamic Text feature to automatically adjust the text size in supported apps. Go to Settings > Display & Brightness > Text Size > Larger Text, and enable the Dynamic Text option.

Display Zoom:

- Allow Display Zoom in Settings > Display & Brightness > Display Zoom to magnify the entire screen and make content appear larger.

Invert Colors and Smart Invert:

- Invert Colors can be helpful for individuals with specific visual impairments. Enable it in Settings > Accessibility > Display & Text Size > Invert Colors.

- Smart Invert is a similar feature that inverts colors but keeps images and media in their original colors. Enable it in Settings > Accessibility > Display & Text Size > Smart Invert.

Reduce Motion:

- Reduce Motion in Settings > Accessibility > Motion to minimize animations and screen transitions, which can be distracting or disorienting for some users.

Tips for Enhancing Hearing Accessibility:

Hearing Aid Compatibility:

- Enable the Hearing Aid Compatibility mode in Settings > Accessibility > Audio/Visual > Hearing Aid Compatibility to improve the audio quality and reduce interference for users with hearing aids.

Mono Audio:

- Enable Mono Audio in Settings > Accessibility > Audio/Visual > Mono Audio to combine stereo audio channels into a single channel, making it easier to hear content if you have hearing loss in one ear.

Custom Audio Settings:

- Adjust audio settings, such as the balance, EQ, and audio routing, to enhance your listening experience. Go to Settings > Accessibility > Audio/Visual > Audio/Visual Accommodations and explore the available options.

Live Listen:

- Use the Live Listen feature with compatible hearing aids or AirPods to turn your iPhone into a remote microphone. Enable it in Settings > Accessibility > Audio/Visual > MFi Hearing Devices > Live Listen.

Subtitles and Closed Captions:

- Enable subtitles or closed captions in supported apps and media players to provide visual text representation of spoken content.

Visual Alerts and Vibrations:

- Enable visual alerts and vibrations for incoming calls, messages, and notifications in Settings > Accessibility > Audio/Visual > LED Flash for Alerts and Vibration options.

CHAPTER 8: Online Safety and Security

Protecting Your Personal Information Online

Strong Passwords:

- Utilize strong and unique passwords for each of your accounts.
- Incorporate a collection of numbers, uppercase and lowercase letters, as well as special characters.
- Avoid using information that is simply guessed, like your name, date of birth, or words that are often utilized.
- It is recommended that you utilize a password manager that can safely store your passwords and create powerful passwords.

Two-Factor Authentication (2FA):

- Allow two-factor authentication whenever available.
- By implementing two-factor authentication, an additional level of security is established as it necessitates a secondary verification step, such as receiving a code on your phone, to gain access to your accounts.

Secure Wi-Fi Networks:

- Use secure Wi-Fi networks with strong encryption when accessing the internet.
- Avoid using public or unsecured Wi-Fi networks, especially when dealing with sensitive information.
- For added security and privacy, it is worth considering the utilization of a virtual private network (VPN).

Be Cautious with Personal Information:

- Personal information should only be shared on trustworthy and secure websites.

- Be wary of requests for personal information through unsolicited emails, messages, or phone calls.
- Review and update your privacy settings on social media networks on a regular basis to minimize the information you publish publicly.

Update Software and Devices:

- Keep your devices, applications and operating systems up to date with the newest security patches and updates.
- Enable automatic updates whenever possible to ensure you have the latest protections against vulnerabilities.

Recognizing and Avoiding Common Scams

Phishing Scams:

- Be cautious of suspicious emails, messages, or websites asking for personal or financial information.
- Exercise care and avoid clicking on links or downloading files from unknown or dubious sources.
- Confirm the validity of requests by contacting the organization through established methods.

Social Engineering:

- Be wary of unsolicited phone calls or texts asking personal or financial information.
- Be wary of requests for money or urgent actions from individuals you don't know personally.
- Double-check the identity of the person or organization before sharing any sensitive information.

Online Shopping Scams:

- Shop from reputable and trusted websites.

- Verify the legitimacy of online sellers and read reviews from other customers.
- Exercise caution when encountering deals that appear excessively advantageous or requests for payment made through insecure methods.

Tech Support Scams:

- Be wary of unsolicited phone calls or pop-up messages purporting to be from technical help.
- Legitimate tech support companies do not proactively contact customers unless previously arranged.
- Under no circumstances should you grant remote access to your computer or disclose personal information to unsolicited callers.

Investment and Financial Scams:

- Research and verify investment opportunities before committing any funds.
- Don't believe claims that huge profits can be made with little risk.
- Seek advice from a reliable financial counselor before making any major financial choices.

Trust Your Instincts:

- If you have a gut feeling that something is amiss or appears too good to be true, it is important to trust your instincts and approach the situation with caution.
- Take the time to research and verify before providing personal information or engaging in financial transactions.

Configuring Privacy Settings on Your iPhone 14

How to Create a Passcode

Passwords on the iPhone are referred to as Passcode. If you need to protect your device from others, here's how to allow a passcode.

1. Go to the Settings menu.
2. Click "Face ID & Passcode" now.

3. Click "Turn On Passcode" from here.

4. Enter your 6-digit passcode or select "Passcode Options" for other options.

5. To confirm, enter the same passcode again.

6. Toggle any option under the "ALLOW ACCESS WHEN LOCKED" heading on or off.

Change Your Password

Here's how to remove your current passcode and replace it with a new one.

1. Go to the Settings menu.

2. Click "Face ID & Passcode" now.

3. If prompted, enter your current passcode.

4. Scroll to the bottom and click "Change Passcode."

5. After that, enter the current passcode.

6. Select "Passcode Options."

7. Make your choice, enter your new passcode, and then re-enter it.

8. Then press the "Done" button.

Disable the Passcode

1. Go to the Settings menu.

2. Click "Face ID & Passcode" now.

3. Select "Turn Passcode Off."

Tips for Creating and Managing Strong Passwords

It is crucial to create and manage strong passwords to safeguard your online accounts and maintain security. Here are some suggestions to assist you in creating and managing strong passwords effectively:

Length and Complexity:

- Select passwords that are at least 12 characters long, as longer passwords provide greater security.

- Ensure your passwords contain a mixture of uppercase and lowercase letters, numbers, and special characters (e.g., !, @, #, $).
- Evade consuming simply recognizable information like your name, birthdate, or common words.
- Consider using a passphrase rather than a single word, such as "MyDog$2Th3Moon!"

Unique Passwords:

- Use a distinct password for each of your online accounts.
- To maintain security across your accounts, it is crucial to avoid reusing passwords. Do not use the same password for multiple accounts, you ensure that if one account is compromised, the security of your other accounts remains intact.

Avoid Predictability:

- Steer clear of using sequential or repeated characters (e.g., 12345678, abcdabcd).
- Avoid common keyboard patterns (e.g., qwerty, asdfg).
- Stay away from using easily guessable information such as your phone number or address.

Password Manager:

- You should think about adopting a password manager service such as "LastPass, 1Password, or Dashlane."
- These programs not only keep your passwords safe but also create robust, one-of-a-kind passwords for every one of your accounts.
- Your password safe may be accessed with only one master password.

Two-Factor Authentication (2FA):

- Whenever possible, enable two-factor authentication.

- This additional security layer requires a second verification step, like a code sent to your phone, to access your account.

Regularly Update Passwords:

- Change your passwords periodically, particularly for sensitive accounts like banking or email.
- Aim to update your passwords at least every 3-6 months or sooner if a security breach occurs.

Be Cautious of Phishing Attempts:

- Exercise caution when dealing with phishing emails, messages, or websites that attempt to deceive you into revealing your passwords.
- Always verify the legitimacy of requests before entering your password or personal information.

Keep Passwords Private:

- It is imperative to never share your passwords with anyone, whether it be friends, family, colleagues, or any other individuals.
- Be cautious when providing passwords over the phone or via email, as legitimate organizations generally do not request them.

Secure Your Devices:

- Utilize strong device passcodes or biometric authentication methods (e.g., fingerprints, Face ID) to protect your devices from unauthorized access.
- Ensure that you lock your devices whenever they are not in use and activate the automatic screen lock feature to initiate after a period of inactivity.

Stay Updated:

- Keep your devices, operating systems, and apps up to date by promptly installing the latest security patches and updates.
- Regularly check for security updates to ensure the highest level of protection.

By following these suggestions, you can create and manage strong passwords that significantly enhance the security of your online accounts. Remember to prioritize unique and complex passwords, consider employing a password manager, and remain vigilant against phishing attempts and unauthorized access.

CHAPTER 9: Troubleshooting and Support

Common Issues and Troubleshooting Solutions

Activation issues

Activation issues are basic when you attempt to get another telephone fully operational just because, paying little mind to show, and the iPhone 14 has demonstrated to be the same

Potential arrangements:

If you're having trouble activating your new iPhone 14, check Apple's System Status page to ensure that all frameworks are ready for action. If something is not turned on the green, wait till all frameworks are up, and then try again. If it's still green and unusable, check to see if your phone has a SIM card embedded. On the off chance that you can switch the SIM card from your old telephone to your new one, try that first. Apple recommends the following steps if you receive a "No SIM" or "Invalid SIM" error msg.

- Ensure your remote arrangement is operational.
- Restart your device after updating to the most recent iOS version.
- Navigate to Setting > General > About. If an update is available, you'll see a prompt to choose OK or Update and then update.
- Remove your SIM card from the plate and replace it. The plate should securely close. Use the plate that came with your current phone, as others may not fit.
- Attempt an alternate SIM card. You can get one at your transporter's retail outlet or request that your bearer test your telephone with an alternate card. Supplant your current SIM card with another one if necessary.

Volume, Sound, and Sound Issues

If you notice that there are issues with any part of sound capacity, there are different cures you can attempt.

Potential arrangements:

- Remove your SIM card from your telephone, and afterward change it to fix the issue of an inadequately situated card.

- Mood killer Bluetooth to contrast sound quality or without it. On the off chance that it improves, leave it off for your calls.

- Ensure your receiver is perfect, clear, and unhindered.

- If the above advances don't improve the sound, clear your telephone's reserved memory by restarting it.

- Do a hard manufacturing plant reset (Settings > General > Reset). Before proceeding to this, make sure to back up your information first.

Bluetooth association issues

Various iPhone 14 users have reported problems connecting their Bluetooth peripherals. The issues include associating, interacting in the vehicle, and maintaining an association after initially interacting. The new iPhone 14 on iOS 16 is experiencing Bluetooth network issues. Associating isn't the problem. The problem is keeping the association together. In addition, I'm experiencing network issues in my vehicle. It will associate for 5 minutes or more before naturally disengaging and reconnecting. It's truly vexing.

Possible arrangements:

- Apple suggests several steps you can take before contacting technical support. Make a point to update your iOS to the most recently released version.

- Go to Settings > Bluetooth on your device then ensure that Bluetooth is turned on. If it is disabled and unable to enable it, restart your iOS device. At that point, try combining and interacting again.

- Ascertain that your Bluetooth frill and device are nearby.

- Turn your Bluetooth frill on and off as needed.

- If your Bluetooth device isn't working, make sure it's switched on, has battery life left, and is plugged in.

- If your extra battery needs to be swapped, try replacing it with new batteries. If you had the option to associate previously, unpair the frill and put it back in revelation mode before attempting to match and interface again.

If you can combine your adornment with different gadgets yet not your iOS gadget, unpair the embellishment from different gadgets and attempt again.

iPhone Won't Turn ON

Whenever you try to turn ON your iPhone, and it doesn't power On, it is either a software or hardware problem.

When faced with the mentioned issue, it is advisable to initially troubleshoot the software on your device as it may be the cause for your iPhone not turning on.

To quickly troubleshoot the software, performing a force reset on your iPhone 14 is recommended. This can be accomplished by following these steps:

1. Press then release the Volume Up button swiftly.

2. Instantly after, press then release the Volume Down button.

3. Lastly, press then grasp the Power button till the device restarts.

Another method to try is a simultaneous press and grasp of the Power and Home buttons till your iPhone 14 powers off and restarts. This action results in a complete shutdown of the device.

If you prefer a non-invasive software fix that does not affect your personal information but resets your Settings app, you can follow these steps:

1. Go to Settings.

2. Select "General."

3. Scroll down and touch "Reset."

4. Choose "Erase All Content and Settings."

5. Enter your passcode and confirm by tapping "Erase iPhone."

6. Your iPhone will restart once the reset process is complete, resolving any software-related issues you may have been experiencing.

In case the problem persists even after attempting the above steps, as a last resort, you may consider performing a DFU (Device Firmware Update) restore. The steps for a DFU restore are outlined below:

- First, connect your iPhone 14 to a PC with iTunes installed.

- Then, hold down the power and home buttons for around 10 seconds until a menu appears.

- After ten secs, still keep holding the *Home button* while you release the Power button.

- You should see detailed information on iTunes on your PC about your device being in recovery mode.

How to Repair iPhone Wi-Fi Problems

Prior to getting in touch with customer support, there are some things that you should check if you have noticed a decrease in the speed of your Wi-Fi connection or an increase in the number of abandoned contacts.

Prior to you start tinkering with the settings of your iPhone 14, you should first determine whether or not the Wi-Fi connection is causing you any difficulties. If you are using the Wi-Fi network in your house, you should try turning off the router for a few moments prior to reconnecting it to the power source.

Whether you are certain that the problem is not caused by the router, you may want to conduct a search to determine whether other individuals in the area who use the similar internet service provider are seeing similar or identical problems.

Go to the Settings app on your iPhone 14 if you are unable to find the router that your mobile phone is connected to or if you are certain that the issue is not related to the connection with your Internet service provider or router.

If you are encountering issues when you have arrived at this location, you will have to verify the Wi-Fi system. Specifically, this is how it should be done:

- In Settings, touch *Wi-Fi*.
- Select your preferred link by touching the "i" icon in the center of the circle. Touch "*Forget this Network*" near the top of the display. (**Note:** This can trigger the request for your Wi-Fi password in your iPhone.)

If this doesn't function, try resetting your iPhone's system settings:

- Head to your "*Settings*" *app*.
- Touch "*General.*"
- Touch *Reset Touch on* Reset Network Settings.

How to Repair iPhone Network Problems

Below are a few things to try if unexpectedly the "No Service" icon appears on your iPhone, and you additionally discover that you cannot connect to your cellular network.

- Before proceeding, it's important to check for any network outages in your area. You can do this by reviewing social media updates or establishing a connection with your service provider through social media channels. Another option is to test the network signal to see if others in your vicinity are facing related problems.
- If the problem appears to be unrelated to a network outage, the next step is to restart your iPhone. Restarting the device can often resolve common issues and restore normal functionality.
- If a restart doesn't solve the problem, you can try enabling Airplane Mode on your iPhone for approximately 30 seconds and then disabling it. This action can

sometimes help in resetting the network settings and resolving connectivity issues.

In the event that you are nevertheless unable to induce it to function regularly, you must attempt shutting off your cellular data totally. To go to your destination, you ought to proceed as follows:

- Navigate to Settings.
- Select Cellular.
- Turn off Cellular Information.
- Toggle it off for one minute, then back on.

Resetting Your iPhone 14 and Restoring Data

Performing Factory Reset

Performing a factory reset on an iPhone restores it to its original state, just as it was when it was first manufactured. This can be beneficial if you are encountering issues with your device and wish to start anew. It is also recommended to carry out a factory reset before selling your iPhone.

However, it is crucial to be aware that performing a factory reset will erase all data on your device, including photos, videos, contacts, text messages, and other files or data stored on the device. Therefore, it is essential to back up any important data before proceeding with the reset process.

To initiate a factory reset on your iPhone 14, follow these steps:

1. Open the Settings app on your device.
2. Scroll down to locate the "Reset" option near the bottom of the list.
3. Touch on the "Reset" option and choose "Erase All Content and Settings."
4. You will be prompted to enter your passcode or use Face ID/Touch ID to confirm your decision to erase everything from your device.

Once you have entered this information correctly, touch "**Erase Now**" at the bottom of the screen and wait for the phone to start clearing everything.

Back Up iPhone

The iPhone may be backed up via iCloud or your PC. To determine which strategy is optimal,

If you replace your iPhone, you may transfer your data to the new device using its backup.

Back Up iPhone Using iCloud

- To access iCloud Backup, go to Settings > [your name] > iCloud > iCloud Backup.
- Enable iCloud Backup.

When your iPhone is on, locked, and connected to Wi-Fi, iCloud will automatically back it up every day.

On 5G-capable iPhone models, your carrier may provide the option to back up your iPhone utilizing the cellular network. Navigate to Settings > [your name] > iCloud > iCloud Backup and toggle Backup Over Cellular on or off.

- To create a backup manually, hit Back Up Now.

Go to Settings > [your name] > iCloud > Manage Account Storage > Backups to see your iCloud backups. Select a backup from the list, then touch Erase & Turn Off Backup to delete it.

Note: If you enable iCloud synchronization for an app or feature (in Settings > [your name] > iCloud > Show All), its data is kept in iCloud. Because the information is automatically updated on all of your devices, it is not backed up to iCloud.

Use Mac To Back Up iPhone

- Cable-connect your iPhone to your PC.
- In the Mac Finder's sidebar, choose your iPhone.

For iPhone backups using the Finder, macOS 10.15 or later is necessary. Earlier versions of macOS need iTunes for iPhone backups.

- At the top of the Finder window, click on "General."
- Next, select the option "Back up all of your iPhone's data to this Mac."
- Select "Encrypt local backup" to encrypt and password-protect your backup data.
- Click Restore Now.

Note: You may also connect your iPhone wirelessly to your computer if you configure syncing via Wi-Fi.

Backup Your iPhone Using A Window

- Cable-connect the iPhone to your PC.
- Click the iPhone button on the top left of the iTunes window on your PC's iTunes program.
- Click Overview.
- Now Click Back Up (below Backups).
- Select "Encrypt local backup," provide a password, and then click Set Password to encrypt your backups.

To see the backups kept on your computer, click Devices after selecting Edit > Preferences. There is a lock symbol next to encrypted backups in the list of backups.

Note: You may also connect your iPhone wirelessly to your computer if you configure syncing via Wi-Fi.

Restore All Content To The iPhone From A Backup

You may restore information, settings, and applications from a backup to a brand-new or recently-deleted iPhone.

Important: Before proceeding, you must build a backup of your iPhone.

Restore iPhone From An iCloud Backup

1. Turn on a brand-new or recently wiped iPhone.

2. Perform one of the subsequent:

- Press Set Up Manually, then touch Restore from iCloud Backup, and then follow the directions on-screen.

- If you have another iPhone, iPad, or iPod touch with iOS 11, iPadOS 13, or a later version, you may use Quick Start to configure your new device immediately. Follow the on-screen prompts to securely replicate many of your settings, preferences, and iCloud Keychain. The remainder of your data and content may then be restored to your new smartphone from your iCloud backup.

Alternatively, if both devices have iOS 12.4, iPadOS 13, or a later version, you may wirelessly transfer all of your data from your former device to your new device. Keep your gadgets close to one another and powered up till the migration is complete.

You need to enter your Apple ID;

Restore iPhone From A Computer Backup

1. Connect a fresh or recently wiped iPhone via USB to the PC storing your backup.

2. Perform one of the subsequent:

- On a Mac (macOS 10.15 or later), pick your iPhone in the Finder sidebar, click Trust, and then click "Restore from this backup."

- On a Mac (macOS 10.14 or older) or a Windows PC: Launch the iTunes application, select the icon resembling an iPhone towards the top left of the iTunes window, then choose Summary, followed by Restore Backup.

Use the most recent version of iTunes.

3. Select your backup from the drop-down menu, then click Continue.

Before restoring your information and settings, you must input the password if your backup is encrypted.

Finding Help through Apple Support Resources

There are multiple methods to reach customer care for the iPhone 14:

1. The first option is to visit the Apple website then click on the "Contact Us" link. This will lead you to a form where you can submit your question or concern. After submitting the form, a customer care representative should respond within 24 hours.

2. Another way to contact iPhone 14 customer care is by calling them directly at 1-800-MY-APPLE (1-800-692-7753). When you dial this number, you will be prompted to choose from a list of options before being connected with a representative who can assist you with your inquiry.

3. Additionally, you have the option to contact customer care through social media platforms like Twitter and Facebook.

4. Simply send them a direct msg detailing your question or concern, and they should reply within 24 hours.

These various communication channels ensure that you have multiple avenues to seek assistance and get the support you need for your iPhone 14.

Connecting with Authorized Service Providers

When it comes to connecting with authorized service providers for your iPhone 14, there are a few avenues you can explore. Here are the steps you can take to find and connect with authorized service providers:

Apple Authorized Service Provider Locator:

1. Visit the Apple Authorized Service Provider Locator website (locate.apple.com) on your computer or smartphone.

2. Enter your location details, such as your city, state, or zip code.

3. Click on the "Go" or "Search" button.

4. You will be presented with a list of authorized service providers in your area.

5. Review the list and find the one that is most convenient for you.

6. Contact the authorized service provider directly to inquire about their services, availability, and any requirements they may have.

Apple Store:

1. If there is an Apple Store near your location, you can visit it in person for assistance.

2. Use the Apple Store app or the Apple website to find the nearest Apple Store.

3. Make an appointment at the Genius Bar or visit the store during their operating hours.

4. The Apple Store staff will evaluate your device and provide guidance on troubleshooting or arrange for service if needed.

It's worth noting that Apple offers limited warranty coverage for its devices. If your iPhone 14 is covered under warranty or you have AppleCare+ protection, you may be eligible for free or discounted repairs. Before seeking service, make sure to check your warranty status to understand your available options.

CHAPTER 10: Advanced Tips and Tricks

Hidden Features and Shortcuts for Efficient Usage

1. Control Center Customization

- Swipe down from the top right corner to access Control Center.

- Touch and grasp on any icon to reveal additional options or settings.

- To customize Control Center, go to Settings > Control Center.

- Touch on "Customize Controls" to add or remove shortcuts for frequently used settings and apps.

- Drag and rearrange the icons to your preferred order.

- You can also add widgets from the Today View by tapping the "+" button.

2. Back Touch

- Go to Settings > Accessibility > Touch > Back Touch.

- Choose "Double Touch" or "Triple Touch" and select an action or shortcut to assign to it.

- For instance, you can assign a double touch to take a screenshot, launch the camera, or activate Siri.

- Once set up, double or triple touch on the back of the iPhone to trigger the assigned action.

3. Reachability

- On iPhones with Face ID, swipe down on the bottom edge of your screen to activate Reachability.

- This brings the top portion of the screen closer to your thumb for easier one-handed use.

- You can touch on any item within Reachability to interact with it.

119

4. Text Selection Tricks

- When editing text, touch and grasp on a word to bring up the selection handles.
- Drag the handles to select a specific portion of text.
- To quickly select a sentence, double-touch on it. Triple-touch to select a paragraph.
- Once selected, you can cut, copy, paste, or apply formatting options from the context menu.

Mastering Siri for Voice Commands and Dictation

1. Hey Siri

- Enable "Hey Siri" in Settings > Siri & Search.
- Set up voice recognition if prompted, or follow the instructions to train Siri to recognize your voice.
- Once enabled, simply say "Hey Siri" followed by your command or question to activate Siri hands-free.

2. Dictation

- When using the keyboard, touch the microphone icon located next to the spacebar.
- This switches the keyboard to dictation mode.
- Speak your msg, and Siri will transcribe it into text.
- You can dictate messages, emails, notes, or search queries without typing.

3. Siri Shortcuts

- Install the Shortcuts app from the App Store if it's not already on your device.
- Open the Shortcuts app and explore the pre-installed shortcuts or create your own.
- To create a custom shortcut, touch the "+" button.

- Follow the prompts to choose actions, set parameters, and customize the voice command or phrase.

- For instance, you can create a shortcut to send a predefined msg to a specific contact or perform a series of actions with a single voice command.

Maximizing Battery Life and Optimizing Performance

1. Low Power Mode

- Enable Low Power Mode in Settings > Battery.

- Low Power Mode reduces background activity, mail fetch, visual effects, and other non-essential functions to conserve battery life.

- You can also enable it through Control Center by swiping down from your the top right corner and tapping on the battery icon.

2. Background App Refresh

- In Settings, go to General > Background App Refresh.

- Here, you can choose which apps are allowed to refresh their content in the background.

- Disable this feature for apps that you don't need to stay up to date constantly, as it can consume battery and data.

3. App Offloading

- If you're running out of storage space, go to Settings > General > iPhone Storage.

- Here, you'll find a list of apps and their respective storage usage.

- Touch on an app you don't frequently use or need and select "Offload App."

- Offloading an app removes the app itself but keeps its data.

- • You can reinstall the app at a later time without losing your data.

Exploring Advanced Camera Functions and Modes

1. Burst Mode

- When capturing action shots, grasp down the shutter button or the volume-up button.

- This activates Burst Mode, which takes a series of photos in rapid succession.

- Release the button to stop capturing.

- Afterward, go to the Photos app to review the burst photos and select the best shot.

2. Night Mode

- On newer iPhone models, the Camera app automatically activates Night Mode in low-light conditions.

- When in a dark environment, grasp the camera steady for a few seconds.

- Night Mode captures multiple images and combines them to create a brighter, more detailed photo.

- You can adjust the exposure time manually by tapping on the Night Mode icon and dragging the slider.

3. ProRAW

- If you're interested in advanced photography and post-processing, enable ProRAW in the Camera settings.

- Open the Camera app, touch on the arrow icon to reveal additional options, and select "ProRAW."

- ProRAW captures images with raw data, providing greater flexibility and control during editing.

- Keep in mind that ProRAW files consume more storage space than standard photos.

4. QuickTake

- While in Photo mode, press and grasp the shutter button.
- This activates QuickTake, allowing you to record a quick video without switching to the Video mode.
- Release the button to stop recording.
- You can swipe right while holding the shutter button to lock the recording and continue without holding the button.

CHAPTER 11: Staying Up to Date with iOS Updates

Understanding iOS Updates and Their Benefits

iOS updates are periodic software releases by Apple that bring new features, improvements, bug fixes, and security enhancements to iPhone devices. These updates ensure that your iPhone remains up to date with the latest advancements and helps optimize its performance and functionality.

There are several benefits to installing iOS updates:

1. New Features: iOS updates often introduce new features and functionalities to enhance the user experience. These can include improvements to existing apps, new app additions, system-level enhancements, or even major interface changes. Upgrading to the latest iOS version allows you to take advantage of these new features and enjoy an enriched iPhone experience.

2. Bug Fixes and Performance Improvements: Software updates address known issues and bugs present in previous iOS versions. By installing updates, you can benefit from bug fixes that enhance the stability, performance, and responsiveness of your iPhone. This can result in smoother operation, fewer crashes, and better overall performance.

3. Security Enhancements: iOS updates often include important security patches that protect your device from vulnerabilities and potential threats. These security updates help safeguard your personal data, prevent unauthorized access, and ensure a safer digital experience. Keeping your iPhone updated with the latest iOS version is crucial for maintaining a secure device.

How to Check for and Install Software Updates

1. Make sure your iPhone 14 is connected to a Wi-Fi network. It is recommended to use Wi-Fi as software updates can be large and may consume a significant amount of cellular data.

2. Touch on the "Settings" app on your iPhone's home screen.

3. Scroll down and touch on "General," which is typically located near the top of the list.

4. Look for and select "Software Update." Your iPhone will check for available updates.

5. If an update is available, click on "Download and Install." If prompted, enter your passcode.

6. Your iPhone will begin downloading the update. Once the download is finished, touch on "Install" then follow the on-screen prompts to complete the installation process.

7. After the installation is finished, your iPhone will restart to apply the update.

Exploring New Features and Improvements

After installing a software update, take the time to explore the new features and improvements that come with it. Apple typically provides release notes or highlights that outline the changes made in the update. Here's how you can explore new features:

- App Updates: Check if any of your installed apps have also been updated. App developers often release updates alongside iOS updates to take advantage of new features or provide compatibility improvements. Open the App Store, go to the "Updates" tab, and install any available app updates.

- System-Level Changes: Apple may introduce new features or make changes to existing system-level functions. Explore the Settings app to see if any new options or settings have been added.

- Apple's Official Resources: Visit Apple's official website, browse through their documentation, or check their release notes to get a complete overview of the changes and new features in the latest iOS update. Apple's website often provides detailed information and guides to help you understand and make the most of the new features.

By staying up to date with iOS updates and exploring their new features, you can make the most of your iPhone's capabilities and ensure that you are benefiting from the latest advancements in Apple's software ecosystem.

CHAPTER 12: Conclusion and Further Resources

Over the years, iPhones have gained a reputation for their extensive features, durability, and high-quality construction, and the new iPhone 14 models uphold this legacy. Throughout this guidebook, we have covered a wide range of topics to help you navigate and make the most of your iPhone 14.

From understanding the evolution of smartphones to exploring the physical features and buttons of the iPhone 14, you have gained a solid foundation of knowledge about your device. We have walked you through the initial setup process, including creating an Apple ID and connecting to Wi-Fi and cellular networks. You have also learned how to personalize your iPhone 14 settings and preferences to tailor it to your liking.

Communication made easy with your iPhone 14 has been discussed extensively, from making and receiving phone calls to sending and receiving text messages. We have explored popular messaging apps like iMessage and WeChat, allowing you to stay connected with friends and family. Additionally, managing contacts and favorites has been covered to help you stay organized.

Capturing and managing photos on your iPhone 14 has been a key topic, from using the Camera app to editing and enhancing your photos. You have also learned how to organize and share your photos through the Photos app and utilize iCloud Photos for backup and synchronization.

The guidebook has introduced you to useful apps and tools specifically designed for seniors, including health and fitness apps, productivity and organization apps, and entertainment and media streaming apps. These apps aim to enhance your daily life and provide hours of enjoyment.

Accessibility features have been highlighted, enabling you to enhance visual and hearing accessibility on your iPhone 14. From VoiceOver and Zoom to Siri for voice control and assistance, you have learned how to make the most of these features.

Online safety and security have been emphasized, with tips on protecting your personal information and recognizing common scams. You have also learned how to configure privacy settings and create strong passwords to safeguard your online accounts.

In case you encounter any issues, troubleshooting solutions and resources for support have been provided. Whether you need to reset your iPhone 14 or seek assistance from Apple support resources or authorized service providers, you will be well-equipped to handle any challenges that may arise.

The guidebook has also touched upon advanced tips and tricks, such as hidden features and shortcuts for efficient usage, maximizing battery life and optimizing performance, and exploring advanced camera functions and modes.

As you continue your journey with your iPhone 14, it's important to stay up to date with iOS updates to benefit from new features and improvements. Regularly checking for and installing software updates will ensure you have the latest enhancements at your fingertips.

In conclusion, the iPhone 14 models offer incremental improvements over their predecessors, and while the differences may not be significant enough to warrant an immediate upgrade, they still represent the cutting-edge technology of Apple's smartphone lineup. As you become more familiar with the several features and capabilities of your iPhone, you will undoubtedly find it to be an exciting and versatile device.

Further Resources

In addition to this guidebook, there are various resources available to further enhance your understanding and proficiency with your iPhone 14. Here are some additional resources you can explore:

- Apple Support Website: The official Apple Support website provides comprehensive guides, tutorials, and troubleshooting tips for all Apple products, including the iPhone. You can find detailed articles, user manuals, and step-by-step instructions to address specific issues or learn more about your device's features. Visit the Apple Support website at support.apple.com.

- Apple User Community: The Apple User Community is an online forum where Apple users from around the world come together to share their experiences, ask questions, and provide solutions. It's a great platform to connect with other iPhone users, learn from their expertise, and discover useful tips and tricks. You can access the Apple User Community at discussions.apple.com.

- Apple Books: Apple Books offers a wide selection of user guides, tutorials, and books specifically written for iPhone users. You can search for titles that cater to your specific needs, whether you're looking for advanced tips, photography techniques, or app recommendations. Access the Apple Books app on your iPhone and search for relevant titles.

- YouTube Tutorials: YouTube is a valuable resource for visual learners. Numerous content creators upload video tutorials and walkthroughs on various iPhone features, tips, and tricks. You can search for specific topics or channels dedicated to iPhone tutorials to find engaging and informative videos that can help you explore your device further.

- Apple Store Workshops: If you prefer hands-on learning experiences, consider attending workshops at your local Apple Store. Apple Stores often offer free workshops on a range of topics, including iPhone basics, photography, accessibility features, and more. These workshops are led by Apple experts who can provide personalized guidance and answer your questions. Check the Apple Store website for workshop schedules and availability.

- Online Courses and Apps: Several online platforms and mobile apps offer courses and interactive lessons on iPhone usage. Websites like Udemy, Coursera, and LinkedIn Learning provide a variety of courses taught by experts in the field. Additionally, apps like Lynda, Skillshare, and SoloLearn offer mobile-friendly lessons and tutorials on iPhone features and functionality.

Remember, exploring and experimenting with your iPhone 14 is the best way to discover its full potential. Don't hesitate to try out different features, apps, and settings to customize your device according to your preferences. The more you engage with your iPhone, the more comfortable and proficient you will become.

Enjoy your iPhone 14 journey, and may these additional resources further enhance your experience and knowledge of your device.

Made in the USA
Las Vegas, NV
23 November 2023